A MIDSUMMER NIGHT'S DREAM

William Shakespeare

A MIDSUMMER NIGHT'S DREAM

A performing edition
by Edward Hall and Roger Warren

OBERON BOOKS
LONDON

First published in this edition in 2003 by Oberon Books Ltd.
(incorporating Absolute Classics)
521 Caledonian Road, London N7 9RH
Tel: 020 7607 3637 / Fax: 020 7607 3629
e-mail: oberon.books@btinternet.com
www.oberonbooks.com

A catalogue record for this book is available from the British Library.

ISBN: 1 84002 363 5

Cover photograph: Manuel Harlan

Printed in Great Britain by Antony Rowe Ltd, Chippenham.

Contents

The Company, 7

The Concord of this Discord, 9

This Edition, 13

A MIDSUMMER NIGHT'S DREAM, 15

The Company

Propeller is an all-male Shakespeare company created at the Watermill Theatre in Newbury. Our aim is simple: to perform Shakespeare's plays with a contemporary aesthetic whilst maintaining the necessary emphasis on the spoken word. For us, developing the relationship between the performer and audience in and around the play is of paramount importance. Most of the problems of directing Shakespeare on the modern stage are created by the indoor theatre. The modern director has to deal with electric lights, a stage that bears no architectural resemblance to the theatre of Shakespeare's day, and a two-act tradition with one interval rather than the classical five-act structure. In producing Shakespeare, Propeller attempts to create some of the atmosphere that must have been a large part of the experience of watching plays in the outdoor theatre. To that end, we use live music played and sung by the actors and are constantly looking for new ways of solving the problems of staging Shakespeare's texts. You may often find that the performance experience begins before you enter the theatre, and continues during the interval, whilst sometimes the action can move in mid-flow from the theatre outside, though not of course in winter…

This company and this text would not exist without the Watermill Theatre. It is vital that the smaller regional producing theatres in this country are financially supported. Grass-roots theatre is the breeding ground for the artists and their work that go on to fill the larger theatres. If we lose many more, our theatre tradition will collapse like a deck of cards, leaving the cultural life of the country substantially poorer.

Edward Hall

The Concord of this Discord

A Midsummer Night's Dream is one of Shakespeare's most original, eloquent, and skilfully constructed works. Although he took hints from various written sources – from Chaucer's *Knight's Tale* and Plutarch's *Lives* for Theseus and Hippolyta, Ovid's *Metamorphoses* for Titania's name and for the mechanicals' play *Pyramus and Thisbe*, perhaps Apuleius' *Golden Ass* for Bottom's transformation – the basic narrative seems, unusually for Shakespeare, to have been his own invention. And although it is a comparatively early play, probably written around 1595, close to *Romeo and Juliet*, which seems to be parodied in the play scene, it is entirely confident in its execution. Largely because of the subject matter and style, it has been suggested that the *Dream* might have been written for the celebration of an Elizabethan court marriage; but if so, it was also given at the public theatres, since the title-page of the first printed edition (1600) says specifically that it was 'sundry times publicly acted …by the Lord Chamberlain's servants', the company to which Shakespeare belonged.

The *Dream* is about love and marriage; and Shakespeare adroitly interweaves four distinct groups of characters – the court, the lovers, the mechanicals, and the fairies – in order to dramatize various aspects of lovers' experience. The wedding of the former adversaries Theseus and Hippolyta is the event towards which the stories of the four groups move, and which finally unites all four in the final scene: the mechanicals have prepared their play *Pyramus and Thisbe* to celebrate the occasion, which also marks the marriages of the four young lovers after their quarrels in the wood, and the resolution of the still more acrimonious strife between Oberon and Titania. The fairies' blessing of the palace at the end of the play is a potent image of the harmony, the 'concord', to which the whole play has been moving.

But that concord has only been achieved by characters who have endured extreme discord. Commenting on the apparently contradictory description of the mechanicals' play as 'very tragical mirth', Theseus asks 'How shall we find the concord of this discord?' The answer seems to be, as always in Shakespearean comedy, to look potential disaster straight in the face. It is as if Shakespeare feels that the resolutions of comedy must be put to the test of harsher experiences if they are to be convincing: the happy ending is the more appreciated if both the characters and the audience are aware of the things that threaten it. Such awareness in no way weakens the humour of the play, but intensifies it by contrast. When Bottom and his companions perform their 'tedious brief scene' before the court, the fatal love of Pyramus and Thisbe is directly relevant to the experience of the four lovers in the wood: without Oberon's benevolent intervention to restore them to their correct pairings, this is how they might have ended up – and an awareness of this may be why they heckle the mechanicals' play so mercilessly.

If the play scene is the climax of the *Dream* as a whole, the climax of the first half is the meeting between Titania and Bottom. Shakespeare's characteristic technique of juxtaposing contrasting extremes is in full operation here, as the fairy queen falls in love with the ass-headed weaver. And in the process the scene contributes to the play's dramatization of love in all its forms: its joys and sadness, its idealism and its selfishness, and the way in which people may fall in love with external appearances – which is why Oberon and Puck squeeze the love-juice on to people's *eyes*. It is typical of the sheer range of the play that it should touch lightly on one extreme of love, the encounter between Beauty and the Beast in the Titania/ Bottom exchange, and yet should also take love on to a higher, more spiritual plane elsewhere. Performing the *Dream* with an all-male cast may help to bring out the a-sexuality, the androgyny in the play, a heightened version of the Elizabethan concern with spiritual relationships between people of the same sex, a spirituality arguably celebrated also in the first 126 of Shakespeare's Sonnets.

Between the extremes of love in the *Dream* stands Theseus. He has had a wild past, including, according to Oberon, an affair with Titania as well as with numerous other mistresses; and he himself acknowledges that he has wooed Hippolyta 'with my sword / And won thy love doing thee injuries'. But now he has become a figure of reason, balanced (possessing a nice sense of irony), a fair law-giver – but a law-giver who can pragmatically bend that law a little when it is in the interests of his subjects to do so. This is made clear in his final judgement on the lovers: towards the end of the play, he does what at the beginning he said he was not able to do, and over-rules Egeus's insistence on the strict application of the Athenian law when he sees that the two pairs of lovers are properly and happily matched.

'The Athenian law': the play, technically, takes place in Athens, and the fairies have come 'from the farthest steppe of India'; but a more English play it would be hard to imagine. This is strikingly apparent in Shakespeare's dramatization of the fairy kingdom. He has taken hints from English folklore for Oberon, Titania, and Puck, but all three are entirely original and individual creations; and they are characterized primarily by means of the language they are given, the famous lyrical writing of the play; but the lyricism is as varied as everything else in the *Dream*. It is primarily used to evoke the rural world which the fairies inhabit and from which they draw their power – from potent natural resources like the wild flowers and the 'fair blessèd beams' of the sun. That relationship is a reciprocal one, and when Oberon and Titania quarrel, nature itself is thrown into chaos. This is the point of the longest, and arguably the finest, speech of the play: Titania's evocation of the bad weather that has resulted from her quarrel with Oberon, a speech which builds to a general confusion of the seasons:

> The spring, the summer,
> The childing autumn, angry winter change
> Their wonted liveries, and the mazèd world
> By their increase now knows not which is which.

But if Titania's speech culminates in such grandeur, it can accommodate much more down-to-earth language too: she can communicate the wretched summer the mortals are enduring by alluding to a rural game, cut out of turf that has now become waterlogged: 'The nine men's morris is filled up with mud.' This muddy image summarizes Shakespeare's daring in this play: the fairy queen, far from being remotely ethereal, expresses herself in terms of everyday country experience. It is this quality which gives the *Dream* its characteristic flavour, and why, despite the references to Athens or India, it seems to be taking place in an English rural community – in, one might say, the Watermill Theatre and its environs, in a wintry world which coexists with a dream of midsummer, an apt reflection of the contrasting extremes dramatized in the play.

Roger Warren

This Edition

This performing edition of *A Midsummer Night's Dream* was prepared for Propeller Productions at the Watermill Theatre, Newbury, and subsequent tour, in 2003. It is based on the first edition, the Quarto text of 1600, almost certainly printed from Shakespeare's manuscript, with a few corrections from the First Folio of 1623. Our text has been planned for an all-male company of twelve actors. The character of Philostrate, Theseus' Master of the Revels, has been omitted entirely, and his speeches reallocated; otherwise, apart from a couple of tiny cuts in Scenes Five and Nine, the text is complete. It has been slightly re-arranged: the speeches of the Fairy in Scene Three have been divided between members of the company; and some of the Court's comments on the mechanicals' play in Scene Nine have been redistributed. The stage directions are based on those of the Quarto.

Our text uses lighter punctuation than strictly grammatical modern usage would require, to preserve the shape and rhythm of the lines as much as possible, and to remove unnecessary obstacles to their speaking. We are very grateful to Angie Kendall for helping to prepare it.

Edward Hall & Roger Warren

A Midsummer Night's Dream is a Propeller Production by the Watermill Theatre. For the Watermill Theatre:

Artistic Director, Jill Fraser

Production Manager, Lawrence T Doyle

Assistant Production Manager, Stuart Harrison

Stage Manager, Rebecca Emery

Deputy Stage Manager, Julia Reid

Assistant Stage Manager, Helen O'Reilly

Wardrobe Supervisors, Sandra Robbs, Corinna Vincent

Marketing Manager, Hannah McKeand

Press Representative, Tei Williams

Production Photographer, Laurence Burns

Following its initial run at the Watermill Theatre, *A Midsummer Night's Dream* was presented at the Holders Festival, Barbados; The Churchill Theatre, Bromley; Cambridge Arts Theatre; The Lowry Arts Centre, Manchester; Yvonne Arnaud Theatre, Guildford; The Hexagon, Reading; The Theatre Royal, Newcastle-upon-Tyne; Richmond Theatre; The Oxford Playhouse; The Globe Theatre, Neuss, Germany; The Comedy Theatre, London.

Characters

THESEUS
Duke of Athens

HIPPOLYTA
Queen of the Amazons

EGEUS

HERMIA
his daughter

DEMETRIUS
rival suitor for Hermia

LYSANDER
rival suitor for Hermia

HELENA
in love with Demetrius

QUINCE
a carpenter

BOTTOM
a weaver

FLUTE
a bellows-mender

STARVELING
a tailor

SNOUT
a tinker

SNUG
a joiner

ROBIN GOODFELLOW
a puck

OBERON
King of the Fairies

TITANIA
Queen of the Fairies

FAIRIES

This edition of *A Midsummer Night's Dream* was first performed at the Watermill Theatre, Newbury on 5 February 2003 with the following cast:

THESEUS, Matthew Flynn

HIPPOLYTA, Emilio Doorgasingh

EGEUS / QUINCE, Christian Myles

HERMIA / SNUG, Jonathan McGuinness

DEMETRIUS / SNOUT, Vincent Leigh

LYSANDER, Dugald Bruce-Lockhart

HELENA, Robert Hands

BOTTOM, Tony Bell

FLUTE, Jules Werner

STARVELING / ROBIN GOODFELLOW,
                                   Simon Scardifield

OBERON, Guy Williams

TITANIA, Richard Clothier

FAIRIES *played by members of the company*

Director, Edward Hall

Designer, Michael Pavelka

Lighting, Ben Ormerod

Music devised and arranged by
    Tony Bell, Jules Werner, and Dugald Bruce-Lockhart

Scene One

Enter THESEUS, HIPPOLYTA, with others.

THESEUS: Now fair Hippolyta, our nuptial hour
    Draws on apace. Four happy days bring in
    Another moon. But oh methinks how slow
    This old moon wanes! She lingers my desires
    Like to a stepdame or a dowager
    Long withering out a young man's revenue.

HIPPOLYTA:
    Four days will quickly steep themselves in night,
    Four nights will quickly dream away the time
    And then the moon like to a silver bow
    New bent in heaven shall behold the night
    Of our solemnities.

THESEUS: Go one of you,
    Stir up the Athenian youth to merriments.
    Awake the pert and nimble spirit of mirth.
    Turn melancholy forth to funerals,
    The pale companion is not for our pomp.
    Hippolyta, I wooed thee with my sword,
    And won thy love doing thee injuries.
    But I will wed thee in another key,
    With pomp, with triumph, and with revelling.

Enter EGEUS and his daughter HERMIA, LYSANDER and DEMETRIUS.

EGEUS: Happy be Theseus, our renownèd Duke.

THESEUS: Thanks good Egeus, what's the news with thee?

EGEUS: Full of vexation come I, with complaint
    Against my child, my daughter Hermia.
    Stand forth Demetrius. My noble lord,
    This man hath my consent to marry her.
    Stand forth Lysander. And my gracious Duke,

This man hath bewitched the bosom of my child.
Thou thou Lysander, thou hast given her rhymes,
And interchanged love tokens with my child.
Thou hast by moonlight at her window sung
With feigning voice verses of feigning love,
And stolen the impression of her fantasy
With bracelets of thy hair, rings, gauds, conceits,
Knacks, trifles, nosegays, sweetmeats – messengers
Of strong prevailment in unhardened youth.
With cunning hast thou filched my daughter's heart,
Turned her obedience which is due to me
To stubborn harshness. And my gracious Duke,
Be it so she will not here before your grace
Consent to marry with Demetrius,
I beg the ancient privilege of Athens:
As she is mine, I may dispose of her,
Which shall be either to this gentleman
Or to her death, according to our law
Immediately provided in that case.

THESEUS: What say you Hermia? Be advised fair maid.
To you your father should be as a god,
One that composed your beauties, yea and one
To whom you are but as a form in wax
By him imprinted and within his power
To leave the figure or disfigure it.
Demetrius is a worthy gentleman.

HERMIA: So is Lysander.

THESEUS: In himself he is,
But in this kind, wanting your father's voice,
The other must be held the worthier.

HERMIA: I would my father looked but with my eyes.

THESEUS: Rather your eyes must with his judgement look.

HERMIA: I do entreat your grace to pardon me.
I know not by what power I am made bold,

Nor how it may concern my modesty
In such a presence here to plead my thoughts,
But I beseech your grace that I may know
The worst that may befall me in this case
If I refuse to wed Demetrius.

THESEUS: Either to die the death, or to abjure
For ever the society of men.
Therefore fair Hermia, question your desires,
Know of your youth, examine well your blood,
Whether if you yield not to your father's choice,
You can endure the livery of a nun,
For aye to be in shady cloister mewed,
To live a barren sister all your life,
Chanting faint hymns to the cold fruitless moon.
Thrice blessèd they that master so their blood
To undergo such maiden pilgrimage;
But earthlier happy is the rose distilled
Than that which withering on the virgin thorn
Grows, lives, and dies in single blessedness.

HERMIA: So will I grow, so live, so die, my lord,
Ere I will yield my virgin patent up
Unto his lordship whose unwishèd yoke
My soul consents not to give sovereignty.

THESEUS: Take time to pause, and by the next new moon,
The sealing day betwixt my love and me
For everlasting bond of fellowship,
Upon that day either prepare to die
For disobedience to your father's will,
Or else to wed Demetrius as he would,
Or on Diana's altar to protest
For aye austerity and single life.

DEMETRIUS: Relent sweet Hermia, and Lysander yield
Thy crazèd title to my certain right.

LYSANDER: You have her father's love, Demetrius;
Let me have Hermia's, do you marry him.

EGEUS: Scornful Lysander, true he hath my love,
 And what is mine my love shall render him,
 And she is mine, and all my right of her
 I do estate unto Demetrius.

LYSANDER: I am, my lord, as well derived as he,
 As well possessed, my love is more than his,
 My fortunes every way as fairly ranked,
 If not with vantage, as Demetrius'.
 And which is more than all these boasts can be,
 I am beloved of beauteous Hermia.
 Why should not I then prosecute my right?
 Demetrius I'll avouch it to his head
 Made love to Nedar's daughter Helena,
 And won her soul, and she sweet lady dotes,
 Devoutly dotes, dotes in idolatry
 Upon this spotted and inconstant man.

THESEUS: I must confess that I have heard so much,
 And with Demetrius thought to have spoke thereof,
 But being over-full of self affairs,
 My mind did lose it. But Demetrius come;
 And come Egeus, you shall go with me.
 I have some private schooling for you both.
 For you fair Hermia, look you arm yourself
 To fit your fancies to your father's will,
 Or else the law of Athens yields you up,
 Which by no means we may extenuate,
 To death or to a vow of single life.
 Come my Hippolyta, what cheer my love?
 Demetrius and Egeus, go along.
 I must employ you in some business
 Against our nuptial, and confer with you
 Of something nearly that concerns yourselves.

EGEUS: With duty and desire we follow you.

 Exeunt all but LYSANDER and HERMIA.

LYSANDER: How now my love, why is your cheek so pale?
How chance the roses there do fade so fast?

HERMIA: Belike for want of rain, which I could well
Beteem them from the tempest of my eyes.

LYSANDER: Ay me, for aught that I could ever read,
Could ever hear by tale or history,
The course of true love never did run smooth,
But either it was different in blood –

HERMIA: O cross, too high to be enthrallèd to low.

LYSANDER: Or else misgraftèd in respect of years –

HERMIA: O spite, too old to be engaged to young.

LYSANDER: Or else it stood upon the choice of friends –

HERMIA: O hell, to choose love by another's eyes.

LYSANDER: Or if there were a sympathy in choice,
War, death or sickness did lay siege to it,
Making it momentary as a sound,
Swift as a shadow, short as any dream,
Brief as the lightning in the collied night,
That in a spleen unfolds both heaven and earth,
And ere a man hath power to say 'behold',
The jaws of darkness do devour it up,
So quick bright things come to confusion.

HERMIA: If then true lovers have been ever crossed,
It stands as an edict in destiny.
Then let us teach our trial patience,
Because it is a customary cross,
As due to love as thoughts and dreams and sighs,
Wishes and tears, poor fancy's followers.

LYSANDER: A good persuasion, therefore hear me Hermia.
I have a widow aunt, a dowager,
Of great revenue and she hath no child,

From Athens is her house remote seven leagues
And she respects me as her only son.
There gentle Hermia, may I marry thee,
And to that place the sharp Athenian law
Cannot pursue us. If thou lov'st me then,
Steal forth thy father's house tomorrow night,
And in the wood a league without the town,
Where I did meet thee once with Helena
To do observance to a morn of May,
There will I stay for thee.

HERMIA: My good Lysander,
I swear to thee by Cupid's strongest bow,
By his best arrow with the golden head,
By the simplicity of Venus' doves,
By that which knitteth souls and prospers loves,
And by that fire which burned the Carthage queen
When the false Trojan under sail was seen,
By all the vows that ever men have broke,
In number more than ever women spoke,
In that same place thou hast appointed me
Tomorrow truly will I meet with thee.

LYSANDER: Keep promise love. Look here comes Helena.

Enter HELENA.

HERMIA: God speed fair Helena, whither away?

HELENA: Call you me fair? That 'fair' again unsay.
Demetrius loves your fair, O happy fair!
Your eyes are lodestars, and your tongue's sweet air
More tuneable than lark to shepherd's ear
When wheat is green, when hawthorn buds appear.
Sickness is catching, O were favour so,
Yours would I catch, fair Hermia, ere I go,
My voice should catch your voice, my eye your eye,
My tongue should catch your tongue's sweet melody.
Were the world mine, Demetrius being bated,

The rest I'll give to be to you translated.
O teach me how you look, and with what art
You sway the motion of Demetrius' heart.

HERMIA: I frown upon him yet he loves me still.

HELENA: O that your frowns would teach my smiles such
skill!

HERMIA: I give him curses yet he gives me love.

HELENA: O that my prayers could such affection move!

HERMIA: The more I hate, the more he follows me.

HELENA: The more I love, the more he hateth me.

HERMIA: His folly, Helena, is no fault of mine.

HELENA: None but your beauty, would that fault were
mine!

HERMIA: Take comfort, he no more shall see my face.
Lysander and myself will fly this place.
Before the time I did Lysander see
Seemed Athens as a paradise to me.
O then what graces in my love do dwell,
That he hath turned a heaven unto a hell?

LYSANDER: Helen, to you our minds we will unfold.
Tomorrow night, when Phoebe doth behold
Her silver visage in the watery glass,
Decking with liquid pearl the bladed grass –
A time that lovers' flights doth still conceal –
Through Athens gates have we devised to steal.

HERMIA: And in the wood where often you and I
Upon faint primrose beds were wont to lie,
Emptying our bosoms of their counsel sweet,
There my Lysander and myself shall meet,
And thence from Athens turn away our eyes
To seek new friends and stranger companies.

Farewell sweet playfellow, pray thou for us,
And good luck grant thee thy Demetrius.
Keep word Lysander, we must starve our sight
From lovers' food till morrow deep midnight. (*Exit.*)

LYSANDER: I will, my Hermia. Helena adieu.
As you on him, Demetrius dote on you. (*Exit.*)

HELENA: How happy some o'er other some can be!
Through Athens I am thought as fair as she.
But what of that? Demetrius thinks not so.
He will not know what all but he do know.
And as he errs, doting on Hermia's eyes,
So I, admiring of his qualities.
Things base and vile, holding no quantity,
Love can transpose to form and dignity.
Love looks not with the eyes but with the mind,
And therefore is winged Cupid painted blind.
Nor hath love's mind of any judgement taste;
Wings and no eyes figure unheedy haste.
And therefore is love said to be a child
Because in choice he is so oft beguiled.
As waggish boys in game themselves forswear,
So the boy Love is perjured everywhere.
For ere Demetrius looked on Hermia's eyne
He hailed down oaths that he was only mine,
And when this hail some heat from Hermia felt,
So he dissolved, and showers of oaths did melt.
I will go tell him of fair Hermia's flight,
Then to the wood will he tomorrow night
Pursue her, and for this intelligence
If I have thanks it is a dear expense.
But herein mean I to enrich my pain,
To have his sight thither and back again. (*Exit.*)

Scene Two

Enter QUINCE the carpenter, and SNUG the joiner, and BOTTOM the weaver, and FLUTE the bellows-mender, and SNOUT the tinker, and STARVELING the tailor.

QUINCE: Is all our company here?

BOTTOM: You were best to call them generally, man by man, according to the scrip.

QUINCE: Here is the scroll of every man's name which is thought fit through all Athens to play in our interlude before the Duke and the Duchess on his wedding day at night.

BOTTOM: First good Peter Quince, say what the play treats on, then read the names of the actors, and so grow to a point.

QUINCE: Marry, our play is the most lamentable comedy and most cruel death of Pyramus and Thisbe.

BOTTOM: A very good piece of work, I assure you, and a merry. Now good Peter Quince, call forth your actors by the scroll. Masters, spread yourselves.

QUINCE: Answer as I call you. Nick Bottom the weaver?

BOTTOM: Ready. Name what part I am for, and proceed.

QUINCE: You, Nick Bottom, are set down for Pyramus.

BOTTOM: What is Pyramus, a lover or a tyrant?

QUINCE: A lover that kills himself most gallant for love.

BOTTOM: That will ask some tears in the true performing of it. If I do it, let the audience look to their eyes. I will move storms. I will condole in some measure. To the rest. Yet my chief humour is for a tyrant. I could play Ercles rarely, or a part to tear a cat in, to make all split.

> The raging rocks
> And shivering shocks
> Shall break the locks
> Of prison gates,
> And Phibbus' car
> Shall shine from far
> And make and mar
> The foolish fates.
> This was lofty. Now name the rest of the players. This is
> Ercles' vein, a tyrant's vein. A lover is more condoling.

QUINCE: Francis Flute the bellows-mender?

FLUTE: Here, Peter Quince.

QUINCE: Flute, you must take Thisbe on you.

FLUTE: What is Thisbe, a wandering knight?

QUINCE: It is the lady that Pyramus must love.

FLUTE: Nay faith, let not me play a woman, I have a beard
coming.

QUINCE: That's all one, you shall play it in a mask, and
you may speak as small as you will.

BOTTOM: An I may hide my face, let me play Thisbe too.
I'll speak in a monstrous little voice: 'Thisne, Thisne!'
'Ah Pyramus, my lover dear, thy Thisbe dear and lady
dear.'

QUINCE: No, no, you must play Pyramus, and Flute, you
Thisbe.

BOTTOM: Well, proceed.

QUINCE: Robin Starveling the tailor?

STARVELING: Here, Peter Quince.

QUINCE: Robin Starveling, you must play Thisbe's
mother. Tom Snout the tinker?

SNOUT: Here, Peter Quince.

QUINCE: You, Pyramus' father, myself Thisbe's father, Snug the joiner, you the lion's part, and I hope here is a play fitted.

SNUG: Have you the lion's part written? Pray you if it be, give it me, for I am slow of study.

QUINCE: You may do it extempore, for it is nothing but roaring.

BOTTOM: Let me play the lion too. I will roar that I will do any man's heart good to hear me. I will roar that I will make the Duke say 'Let him roar again, let him roar again.'

QUINCE: If you should do it too terribly you would fright the Duchess and the ladies that they would shriek, and that were enough to hang us all.

ALL: That would hang us, every mother's son.

BOTTOM: I grant you, friends, if you should fright the ladies out of their wits they would have no more discretion but to hang us, but I will aggravate my voice so that I will roar you as gently as any sucking dove, I will roar you an 'twere any nightingale.

QUINCE: You can play no part but Pyramus. For Pyramus is a sweet-faced man, a proper man as one shall see in a summer's day, a most lovely gentlemanlike man, therefore you must needs play Pyramus.

BOTTOM: Well, I will undertake it. What beard were I best to play it in?

QUINCE: Why, what you will.

BOTTOM: I will discharge it in either your straw-colour beard, your orange-tawny beard, your purple-in-grain beard, or your French-crown-colour beard, your perfect yellow.

QUINCE: Some of your French crowns have no hair at all, and then you will play bare-faced. But masters, here are your parts, and I am to entreat you, request you, and desire you to con them by tomorrow night, and meet me in the palace wood a mile without the town by moonlight. There will we rehearse, for if we meet in the city we shall be dogged with company, and our devices known. In the meantime I will draw a bill of properties such as our play wants. I pray you fail me not.

BOTTOM: We will meet, and there we may rehearse most obscenely and courageously. Take pains, be perfect, adieu.

QUINCE: At the Duke's oak we meet.

BOTTOM: Enough, hold or cut bowstrings.

Exeunt.

Scene Three

Enter FAIRIES at one door and ROBIN GOODFELLOW, a puck, at another.

ROBIN: How now spirits, whither wander you?

FAIRIES: Over hill, over dale,
　　Thorough bush, thorough briar,
　　Over park, over pale,
　　Thorough flood, thorough fire:
　　I do wander everywhere
　　Swifter than the moon's sphere,
　　And I serve the fairy queen
　　To dew her orbs upon the green.
　　The cowslips tall her pensioners be,
　　In their gold coats spots you see:
　　Those be rubies, fairy favours,
　　In those freckles live their savours.

I must go seek some dewdrops here,
And hang a pearl in every cowslip's ear.
Farewell thou lob of spirits, I'll be gone,
Our queen and all her elves come here anon.

ROBIN: The king doth keep his revels here tonight.
Take heed the queen come not within his sight,
For Oberon is passing fell and wroth
Because that she as her attendant hath
A lovely boy stolen from an Indian king:
She never had so sweet a changeling.
And jealous Oberon would have the child
Knight of his train to trace the forests wild.
But she perforce withholds the lovèd boy,
Crowns him with flowers and makes him all her joy.
And now they never meet in grove or green,
By fountain clear or spangled starlight sheen,
But they do square, that all their elves for fear
Creep into acorn cups and hide them there.

FAIRIES: Either I mistake your shape and making quite
Or else you are that shrewd and knavish sprite
Called Robin Goodfellow. Are not you he
That frights the maidens of the villagery,
Skim milk, and sometimes labour in the quern,
And bootless make the breathless housewife churn,
And sometime make the drink to bear no barm,
Mislead night wanderers, laughing at their harm?
Those that hobgoblin call you, and 'sweet puck',
You do their work, and they shall have good luck.
Are not you he?

ROBIN: Thou speak'st aright;
I am that merry wanderer of the night.
I jest to Oberon and make him smile
When I a fat and bean-fed horse beguile,
Neighing in likeness of a filly foal;
And sometime lurk I in a gossip's bowl

In very likeness of a roasted crab,
And when she drinks, against her lips I bob,
And on her withered dewlap pour the ale.
The wisest aunt telling the saddest tale
Sometime for three-foot stool mistaketh me;
Then slip I from her bum, down topples she,
And 'tailor' cries, and falls into a cough,
And then the whole choir hold their hips and laugh,
And waxen in their mirth, and sneeze, and swear
A merrier hour was never wasted there.
But room, fairy, here comes Oberon.

FAIRY: And here my mistress, would that he were gone.

*Enter OBERON the King of Fairies at one door with his
train, and TITANIA the Queen at another with hers.*

OBERON: Ill met by moonlight, proud Titania.

TITANIA: What, jealous Oberon! Fairies skip hence.
I have forsworn his bed and company.

OBERON: Tarry rash wanton, am not I thy lord?

TITANIA: Then I must be thy lady; but I know
When thou hast stolen away from fairyland
And in the shape of Corin sat all day,
Playing on pipes of corn and versing love
To amorous Phillida. Why art thou here
Come from the farthest steppe of India,
But that, forsooth, the bouncing Amazon,
Your buskined mistress and your warrior love,
To Theseus must be wedded, and you come
To give their bed joy and prosperity?

OBERON: How canst thou thus for shame, Titania,
Glance at my credit with Hippolyta,
Knowing I know thy love to Theseus?
Didst not thou lead him through the glimmering night
From Perigenia whom he ravishèd,

And make him with fair Aegles break his faith,
With Ariadne and Antiopa?

TITANIA: These are the forgeries of jealousy,
And never since the middle summer's spring
Met we on hill, in dale, forest or mead,
By pavèd fountain or by rushy brook,
Or in the beachèd margin of the sea
To dance our ringlets to the whistling wind,
But with thy brawls thou hast disturbed our sport.
Therefore the winds, piping to us in vain,
As in revenge have sucked up from the sea
Contagious fogs which falling in the land
Hath every pelting river made so proud
That they have overborne their continents.
The ox hath therefore stretched his yoke in vain,
The ploughman lost his sweat, and the green corn
Hath rotted ere his youth attained a beard.
The fold stands empty in the drownèd field,
And crows are fatted with the murrion flock.
The nine men's morris is filled up with mud,
And the quaint mazes in the wanton green
For lack of tread are undistinguishable.
The human mortals want their winter cheer,
No night is now with hymn or carol blest.
Therefore the moon, the governess of floods,
Pale in her anger washes all the air
That rheumatic diseases do abound.
And thorough this distemperature we see
The seasons alter: hoary-headed frosts
Fall in the fresh lap of the crimson rose,
And on old Hiems' thin and icy crown
An odorous chaplet of sweet summer buds
Is as in mockery set. The spring, the summer,
The childing autumn, angry winter change
Their wonted liveries, and the mazèd world
By their increase now knows not which is which.

And this same progeny of evils comes
From our debate, from our dissension.
We are their parents and original.

OBERON: Do you amend it then, it lies in you.
Why should Titania cross her Oberon?
I do but beg a little changeling boy
To be my henchman.

TITANIA: Set your heart at rest.
The fairy land buys not the child of me.
His mother was a votaress of my order,
And in the spicèd Indian air by night
Full often hath she gossiped by my side,
And sat with me on Neptune's yellow sands,
Marking th'embarkèd traders on the flood,
When we have laughed to see the sails conceive
And grow big-bellied with the wanton wind,
Which she with pretty and with swimming gait
Following, her womb then rich with my young squire,
Would imitate, and sail upon the land
To fetch me trifles, and return again
As from a voyage rich with merchandise.
But she, being mortal, of that boy did die;
And for her sake do I rear up her boy;
And for her sake I will not part with him.

OBERON: How long within this wood intend you stay?

TITANIA: Perchance till after Theseus' wedding day.
If you will patiently dance in our round,
And see our moonlight revels, go with us.
If not, shun me, and I will spare your haunts.

OBERON: Give me that boy and I will go with thee.

TITANIA: Not for thy fairy kingdom. Fairies, away.
We shall chide downright if I longer stay.

Exeunt TITANIA and her train.

OBERON: Well go thy way, thou shalt not from this grove
    Till I torment thee for this injury.
    My gentle puck, come hither. Thou rememb'rest
    Since once I sat upon a promontory
    And heard a mermaid on a dolphin's back
    Uttering such dulcet and harmonious breath
    That the rude sea grew civil at her song
    And certain stars shot madly from their spheres
    To hear the sea-maid's music?

ROBIN: I remember.

OBERON: That very time I saw, but thou couldst not,
    Flying between the cold moon and the earth
    Cupid all armed. A certain aim he took
    At a fair vestal thronèd by the west,
    And loosed his love-shaft smartly from his bow
    As it should pierce a hundred thousand hearts.
    But I might see young Cupid's fiery shaft
    Quenched in the chaste beams of the watery moon,
    And the imperial votaress passed on,
    In maiden meditation, fancy free.
    Yet marked I where the bolt of Cupid fell.
    It fell upon a little western flower
    Before milk-white, now purple with love's wound,
    And maidens call it love-in-idleness.
    Fetch me that flower; the herb I showed thee once.
    The juice of it on sleeping eyelids laid
    Will make or man or woman madly dote
    Upon the next live creature that it sees.
    Fetch me this herb, and be thou here again
    Ere the leviathan can swim a league.

ROBIN: I'll put a girdle round about the earth
    In forty minutes. (*Exit.*)

OBERON: Having once this juice,
    I'll watch Titania when she is asleep,
    And drop the liquor of it in her eyes.
    The next thing then she waking looks upon,
    Be it on lion, bear, or wolf, or bull,
    On meddling monkey or on busy ape,
    She shall pursue it with the soul of love.
    And ere I take this charm from off her sight,
    As I can take it with another herb,
    I'll make her render up her page to me.
    But who comes here? I am invisible,
    And I will overhear their conference.

Enter DEMETRIUS, HELENA following him.

DEMETRIUS: I love thee not, therefore pursue me not.
    Where is Lysander, and fair Hermia?
    The one I'll slay, the other slayeth me.
    Thou told'st me they were stolen unto this wood,
    And here am I, and wood within this wood,
    Because I cannot meet my Hermia.
    Hence get thee gone, and follow me no more.

HELENA: You draw me, you hard-hearted adamant,
    But yet you draw not iron, for my heart
    Is true as steel. Leave you your power to draw,
    And I shall have no power to follow you.

DEMETRIUS: Do I entice you, do I speak you fair,
    Or rather do I not in plainest truth
    Tell you I do not nor I cannot love you?

HELENA: And even for that do I love you the more.
    I am your spaniel, and Demetrius,
    The more you beat me I will fawn on you.
    Use me but as your spaniel: spurn me, strike me,
    Neglect me, lose me; only give me leave,
    Unworthy as I am, to follow you.
    What worser place can I beg in your love,

And yet a place of high respect with me,
Than to be usèd as you use your dog?

DEMETRIUS: Tempt not too much the hatred of my spirit,
For I am sick when I do look on thee.

HELENA: And I am sick when I look not on you.

DEMETRIUS: You do impeach your modesty too much,
To leave the city and commit yourself
Into the hands of one that loves you not,
To trust the opportunity of night,
And the ill counsel of a desert place,
With the rich worth of your virginity.

HELENA: Your virtue is my privilege for that.
It is not night when I do see your face,
Therefore I think I am not in the night,
Nor doth this wood lack worlds of company,
For you in my respect are all the world.
Then how can it be said I am alone,
When all the world is here to look on me?

DEMETRIUS: I'll run from thee and hide me in the brakes,
And leave thee to the mercy of wild beasts.

HELENA: The wildest hath not such a heart as you.
Run when you will, the story shall be changed:
Apollo flies, and Daphne holds the chase.
The dove pursues the griffin, the mild hind
Makes speed to catch the tiger: bootless speed,
When cowardice pursues and valour flies.

DEMETRIUS: I will not stay thy questions, let me go;
Or if thou follow me, do not believe
But I shall do thee mischief in the wood.

HELENA: Ay, in the temple, in the town, the field,
You do me mischief. Fie Demetrius,
Your wrongs do set a scandal on my sex.

We cannot fight for love as men may do;
We should be wooed, and were not made to woo.
I'll follow thee and make a heaven of hell,
To die upon the hand I love so well.

Exit DEMETRIUS, HELENA following him.

OBERON: Fare thee well nymph, ere he do leave this grove
Thou shalt fly him, and he shall seek thy love.

Enter ROBIN.

Hast thou the flower there? Welcome wanderer.

ROBIN: Ay, there it is.

OBERON: I pray thee give it me.
I know a bank where the wild thyme blows,
Where oxlips and the nodding violet grows,
Quite overcanopied with luscious woodbine,
With sweet musk-roses and with eglantine.
There sleeps Titania sometime of the night,
Lulled in these flowers with dances and delight;
And there the snake throws her enamelled skin,
Weed wide enough to wrap a fairy in.
And with the juice of this I'll streak her eyes,
And make her full of hateful fantasies.
Take thou some of it, and seek through this grove.
A sweet Athenian lady is in love
With a disdainful youth; anoint his eyes,
But do it when the next thing he espies
May be the lady. Thou shalt know the man
By the Athenian garments he hath on.
Effect it with some care, that he may prove
More fond on her than she upon her love,
And look thou meet me ere the first cock crow.

ROBIN: Fear not, my lord, your servant shall do so.

Exeunt.

Scene Four

Enter TITANIA Queen of Fairies with her train.

TITANIA: Come now a roundel and a fairy song.
　　Then for the third part of a minute hence,
　　Some to kill cankers in the musk-rose buds,
　　Some war with reremice for their leathern wings
　　To make my small elves coats, and some keep back
　　The clamorous owl that nightly hoots and wonders
　　At our quaint spirits. Sing me now asleep;
　　Then to your offices, and let me rest.

　　FAIRIES sing.

FAIRIES: You spotted snakes with double tongue,
　　Thorny hedgehogs, be not seen,
　　Newts and blindworms, do no wrong,
　　Come not near our fairy queen.
　　Philomel with melody,
　　Sing in our sweet lullaby,
　　Lulla, lulla, lullaby, lulla, lulla, lullaby.
　　Never harm
　　Nor spell nor charm
　　Come our lovely lady nigh.
　　So good night, with lullaby.
　　Weaving spiders, come not here,
　　Hence you long-legged spinners, hence;
　　Beetles black, approach not near;
　　Worm nor snail do no offence.

　　Philomel with melody, *(Etc.)*

FAIRY: Hence away, now all is well.
　　One aloof stand sentinel.

　　She sleeps. Exeunt FAIRIES. Enter OBERON.

OBERON: What thou seest when thou dost wake,
　　Do it for thy true love take;

37

Love and languish for his sake.
Be it ounce or cat or bear,
Pard or boar with bristled hair,
In thy eye that shall appear
When thou wak'st, it is thy dear.
Wake when some vile thing is near. (*Exit.*)

Enter LYSANDER and HERMIA.

LYSANDER: Fair love, you faint with wandering in the wood,
And to speak truth, I have forgot our way.
We'll rest us Hermia, if you think it good,
And tarry for the comfort of the day.

HERMIA: Be it so Lysander, find you out a bed;
For I upon this bank will rest my head.

LYSANDER: One turf shall serve as pillow for us both,
One heart, one bed, two bosoms, and one troth.

HERMIA: Nay good Lysander, for my sake my dear,
Lie further off yet, do not lie so near.

LYSANDER: O take the sense, sweet, of my innocence.
Love takes the meaning in love's conference.
I mean that my heart unto yours is knit,
So that but one heart we can make of it.
Two bosoms interchainèd with an oath,
So then two bosoms and a single troth.
Then by your side no bed-room me deny,
For lying so, Hermia, I do not lie.

HERMIA: Lysander riddles very prettily.
Now much beshrew my manners and my pride
If Hermia meant to say Lysander lied.
But gentle friend, for love and courtesy,
Lie further off in human modesty.
Such separation as may well be said
Becomes a virtuous bachelor and a maid,
So far be distant, and good night sweet friend.
Thy love ne'er alter till thy sweet life end.

LYSANDER: Amen amen to that fair prayer say I,
    And then end life when I end loyalty.
    Here is my bed; sleep give thee all his rest.

HERMIA: With half that wish the wisher's eyes be pressed.

They sleep. Enter ROBIN.

ROBIN: Through the forest have I gone,
    But Athenian found I none
    On whose eyes I might approve
    This flower's force in stirring love.
    Night and silence. Who is here?
    Weeds of Athens he doth wear.
    This is he my master said
    Despisèd the Athenian maid.
    And here the maiden sleeping sound
    On the dank and dirty ground.
    Pretty soul, she durst not lie
    Near this lack-love, this kill-courtesy.
    Churl, upon thy eyes I throw
    All the power this charm doth owe.
    When thou wak'st let love forbid
    Sleep his seat on thy eyelid.
    So awake when I am gone,
    For I must now to Oberon. (*Exit.*)

Enter DEMETRIUS and HELENA, running.

HELENA: Stay though thou kill me, sweet Demetrius.

DEMETRIUS: I charge thee hence and do not haunt me thus.

HELENA: O wilt thou darkling leave me? Do not so.

DEMETRIUS: Stay on thy peril; I alone will go. (*Exit.*)

HELENA: O I am out of breath in this fond chase.
    The more my prayer, the lesser is my grace.
    Happy is Hermia, wheresoe'er she lies,
    For she hath blessèd and attractive eyes.

How came her eyes so bright? Not with salt tears;
If so, my eyes are oftener washed than hers.
No, no, I am as ugly as a bear,
For beasts that meet me run away for fear.
Therefore no marvel though Demetrius
Do as a monster fly my presence thus.
What wicked and dissembling glass of mine
Made me compare with Hermia's sphery eyne!
But who is here? Lysander, on the ground?
Dead or asleep? I see no blood, no wound.
Lysander, if you live, good sir awake.

LYSANDER: And run through fire I will for thy sweet sake.
Transparent Helena, nature shows her art
That through thy bosom makes me see thy heart.
Where is Demetrius? O how fit a word
Is that vile name to perish on my sword!

HELENA: Do not say so, Lysander, say not so.
What though he love your Hermia? Lord, what though?
Yet Hermia still loves you, then be content.

LYSANDER: Content with Hermia? No, I do repent
The tedious minutes I with her have spent.
Not Hermia but Helena I love.
Who will not change a raven for a dove?
The will of man is by his reason swayed,
And reason says you are the worthier maid.
Things growing are not ripe until their season,
So I, being young, till now ripe not to reason,
And touching now the point of human skill,
Reason becomes the marshal to my will,
And leads me to your eyes, where I o'erlook
Love's stories written in love's richest book.

HELENA: Wherefore was I to this keen mockery born?
When at your hands did I deserve this scorn?
Is't not enough, is't not enough, young man,

That I did never, no nor never can
Deserve a sweet look from Demetrius' eye,
But you must flout my insufficiency?
Good troth you do me wrong, good sooth you do,
In such disdainful manner me to woo.
But fare you well, perforce I must confess
I thought you lord of more true gentleness.
O that a lady of one man refused
Should of another therefore be abused! (*Exit.*)

LYSANDER: She sees not Hermia. Hermia sleep thou there,
And never mayst thou come Lysander near;
For as a surfeit of the sweetest things
The deepest loathing to the stomach brings,
Or as the heresies that men do leave
Are hated most of those they did deceive,
So thou, my surfeit and my heresy,
Of all be hated, but the most of me;
And all my powers, address your love and might
To honour Helen, and to be her knight. (*Exit.*)

HERMIA: Help me Lysander, help me, do thy best
To pluck this crawling serpent from my breast.
Ay me for pity, what a dream was here?
Lysander, look how I do quake with fear.
Methought a serpent ate my heart away,
And you sat smiling at his cruel prey.
Lysander! What, removed? Lysander lord,
What out of hearing gone? No sound, no word?
Alack where are you? Speak an if you hear,
Speak, of all loves, I swoon almost with fear.
No? Then I well perceive you are not nigh.
Either death or you I'll find immediately. (*Exit.*)

Scene Five

Enter the clowns: BOTTOM, QUINCE, FLUTE, SNOUT, STARVELING, and SNUG.

BOTTOM: Are we all met?

QUINCE: Pat, pat, and here's a marvellous convenient place for our rehearsal. This green plot shall be our stage, this hawthorn brake our tiring-house, and we will do it in action as we will do it before the Duke.

BOTTOM: Peter Quince.

QUINCE: What sayst thou, bully Bottom?

BOTTOM: There are things in this comedy of Pyramus and Thisbe that will never please. First, Pyramus must draw a sword to kill himself, which the ladies cannot abide. How answer you that?

SNOUT: By 'r lakin, a parlous fear.

STARVELING: I believe we must leave the killing out, when all is done.

BOTTOM: Not a whit. I have a device to make all well. Write me a prologue, and let the prologue seem to say we will do no harm with our swords, and that Pyramus is not killed indeed; and for the more better assurance, tell them that I Pyramus am not Pyramus, but Bottom the weaver. This will put them out of fear.

QUINCE: Well, we will have such a prologue, and it shall be written in eight and six.

BOTTOM: No, make it two more, let it be written in eight and eight.

SNOUT: Will not the ladies be afeard of the lion?

STARVELING: I fear it, I promise you.

BOTTOM: Masters, you ought to consider with yourselves, to bring in, God shield us, a lion among ladies is a most dreadful thing; for there is not a more fearful wild fowl than your lion living, and we ought to look to't.

SNOUT: Therefore another prologue must tell he is not a lion.

BOTTOM: Nay, you must name his name, and half his face must be seen through the lion's neck, and he himself must speak through, saying thus or to the same defect: 'ladies', or 'fair ladies, I would wish you' or 'I would request you' or 'I would entreat you, not to fear, not to tremble, my life for yours: if you think I come hither as a lion, it were pity of my life. No, I am no such thing, I am a man, as other men are,' and there indeed let him name his name and tell them plainly he is Snug the joiner.

QUINCE: Well, it shall be so; but there is two hard things: that is, to bring the moonlight into a chamber, for you know Pyramus and Thisbe meet by moonlight.

SNUG: Doth the moon shine that night we play our play?

BOTTOM: A calendar, a calendar, look in the almanac, find out moonshine, find out moonshine.

QUINCE: Yes, it doth shine that night.

BOTTOM: Why then may you leave a casement of the great chamber window where we play open, and the moon may shine in at the casement.

QUINCE: Ay, or else one must come in with a bush of thorns and a lantern, and say he comes to disfigure or to present the person of Moonshine. Then there is another thing: we must have a wall in the great chamber, for Pyramus and Thisbe, says the story, did talk through the chink of a wall.

SNOUT: You can never bring in a wall. What say you, Bottom?

BOTTOM: Some man or other must present wall; and let him have some plaster or some loam or some rough-cast about him to signify wall, and let him hold his fingers thus, and through that cranny shall Pyramus and Thisbe whisper.

QUINCE: If that may be, then all is well. Come sit down every mother's son, and rehearse your parts. Pyramus, you begin. When you have spoken your speech, enter into that brake, and so everyone according to his cue.

Enter ROBIN.

ROBIN: What hempen homespuns have we swaggering here
So near the cradle of the fairy queen?
What, a play toward? I'll be an auditor,
An actor too perhaps if I see cause.

QUINCE: Speak Pyramus. Thisbe stand forth.

BOTTOM: 'Thisbe, the flowers of odious savours sweet' –

QUINCE: Odours, odours.

BOTTOM: ' – odours savours sweet.
So hath thy breath, my dearest Thisbe dear.
But hark, a voice. Stay thou but here a while,
And by and by I will to thee appear.' (*Exit.*)

ROBIN: A stranger Pyramus than e'er played here. (*Exit.*)

FLUTE: Must I speak now?

QUINCE: Ay marry must you, for you must understand he goes but to see a noise that he heard, and is to come again.

FLUTE: 'Most radiant Pyramus, most lily-white of hue,
Of colour like the red rose on triumphant briar,

Most brisky juvenile, and eke most lovely jew,
As true as truest horse that yet would never tire,
I'll meet thee, Pyramus, at Ninny's tomb.'

QUINCE: Ninus' tomb, man! Why you must not speak
that yet, that you answer to Pyramus. You speak all
your part at once, cues and all. Pyramus enter: your
cue is past; it is 'never tire'.

FLUTE: O, 'As true as truest horse that yet would never tire.'

Enter BOTTOM with the ass-head, and ROBIN.

BOTTOM: 'If I were fair, Thisbe, I were only thine.'

QUINCE: O monstrous! O strange! We are haunted. Pray
masters, fly masters: help!

The clowns all exit.

ROBIN: I'll follow you, I'll lead you about a round,
Through bog, through bush, through brake, through briar.
Sometime a horse I'll be, sometime a hound,
A hog, a headless bear, sometime a fire,
And neigh and bark and grunt and roar and burn,
Like horse, hound, hog, bear, fire, at every turn. (*Exit.*)

BOTTOM: Why do they run away? This is a knavery of
them to make me afeard.

Enter SNOUT.

SNOUT: O Bottom, thou art changed. What do I see on
thee?

BOTTOM: What do you see? You see an ass-head of your
own, do you?

Exit SNOUT.

Enter QUINCE.

QUINCE: Bless thee Bottom, bless thee. Thou art
translated. (*Exit.*)

BOTTOM: I see their knavery. This is to make an ass of me,
to fright me if they could; but I will not stir from this
place, do what they can. I will walk up and down here,
and I will sing that they shall hear I am not afraid.
The wousel cock so black of hue,
With orange-tawny bill;
The throstle with his note so true,
The wren with little quill.

TITANIA: What angel wakes me from my flowery bed?

BOTTOM: The finch, the sparrow, and the lark,
The plainsong cuckoo grey,
Whose note full many a man doth mark,
And dares not answer 'nay'.

TITANIA: I pray thee gentle mortal, sing again.
Mine ear is much enamoured of thy note;
So is mine eye enthrallèd to thy shape;
And thy fair virtue's force perforce doth move me
On the first view to say, to swear, I love thee.

BOTTOM: Methinks mistress, you should have little reason
for that. And yet to say the truth, reason and love keep
little company together nowadays; the more the pity that
some honest neighbours will not make them friends.
Nay, I can gleek upon occasion.

TITANIA: Thou art as wise as thou art beautiful.

BOTTOM: Not so neither, but if I had wit enough to get out
of this wood, I have enough to serve mine own turn.

TITANIA: Out of this wood do not desire to go.
Thou shalt remain here, whether thou wilt or no.
I am a spirit of no common rate:
The summer still doth tend upon my state,
And I do love thee, therefore go with me.
I'll give thee fairies to attend on thee,
And they shall fetch thee jewels from the deep,

And sing while thou on pressèd flowers dost sleep,
And I will purge thy mortal grossness so
That thou shalt like an airy spirit go.
Peaseblossom, Cobweb, Moth, and Mustardseed!

Enter the four FAIRIES.

PEASEBLOSSOM: Ready.

COBWEB: And I.

MOTH: And I.

MUSTARDSEED: And I.

ALL FOUR: Where shall we go?

TITANIA: Be kind and courteous to this gentleman.
Hop in his walks, and gambol in his eyes,
Feed him with apricocks and dewberries,
With purple grapes, green figs, and mulberries;
The honeybags steal from the humble-bees,
And for night tapers crop their waxen thighs
And light them at the fiery glow-worms' eyes
To have my love to bed, and to arise;
And pluck the wings from painted butterflies
To fan the moonbeams from his sleeping eyes.
Nod to him elves, and do him courtesies.

PEASEBLOSSOM: Hail, mortal.

COBWEB: Hail.

MOTH: Hail.

MUSTARDSEED: Hail.

BOTTOM: I cry your worship's mercy, heartily. I beseech
your worship's name.

COBWEB: Cobweb.

BOTTOM: I shall desire you of more acquaintance, good Master Cobweb. If I cut my finger, I shall make bold with you. Your name, honest gentleman?

PEASEBLOSSOM: Peaseblossom.

BOTTOM: I pray you commend me to Mistress Squash your mother, and to Master Peascod your father. Good Master Peaseblossom, I shall desire you of more acquaintance, too. Your name, I beseech you, sir?

MUSTARDSEED: Mustardseed.

BOTTOM: Good Master Mustardseed, I know your patience well. That same cowardly giantlike ox-beef hath devoured many a gentleman of your house. I promise you your kindred hath made my eyes water ere now. I desire your more acquaintance, good Master Mustardseed.

TITANIA: Come wait upon him, lead him to my bower.
The moon, methinks, looks with a watery eye,
And when she weeps, weeps every little flower,
Lamenting some enforcèd chastity.
Tie up my lover's tongue, bring him silently.

Exeunt.

Interval.

Scene Six

Enter OBERON, King of Fairies.

OBERON: I wonder if Titania be awaked,
    Then what it was that next came in her eye,
    Which she must dote on in extremity.

Enter ROBIN GOODFELLOW.

    Here comes my messenger. How now, mad spirit?
    What night-rule now about this haunted grove?

ROBIN: My mistress with a monster is in love.
    Near to her close and consecrated bower
    While she was in her dull and sleeping hour
    A crew of patches, rude mechanicals
    That work for bread upon Athenian stalls,
    Were met together to rehearse a play
    Intended for great Theseus' nuptial day.
    The shallowest thickskin of that barren sort,
    Who Pyramus presented in their sport,
    Forsook his scene and entered in a brake,
    When I did him at this advantage take:
    An ass's nole I fixèd on his head.
    Anon his Thisbe must be answerèd,
    And forth my mimic comes. When they him spy,
    As wild geese that the creeping fowler eye,
    Or russet-pated choughs, many in sort,
    Rising and cawing at the gun's report,
    Sever themselves and madly sweep the sky,
    So at his sight away his fellows fly,
    And at our stamp here o'er and o'er one falls.
    He 'murder' cries, and help from Athens calls.
    Their sense thus weak, lost with their fears thus strong,
    Made senseless things begin to do them wrong.
    For briars and thorns at their apparel snatch;
    Some sleeves, some hats: from yielders all things catch.
    I led them on in this distracted fear,

And left sweet Pyramus translated there,
When in that moment, so it came to pass,
Titania waked and straightway loved an ass.

OBERON: This falls out better than I could devise.
But hast thou yet latched the Athenian's eyes
With the love juice, as I did bid thee do?

ROBIN: I took him sleeping, that is finished, too;
And the Athenian woman by his side,
That when he waked, of force she must be eyed.

Enter DEMETRIUS and HERMIA.

OBERON: Stand close, this is the same Athenian.

ROBIN: This is the woman, but not this the man.

DEMETRIUS: O why rebuke you him that loves you so?
Lay breath so bitter on your bitter foe.

HERMIA: Now I but chide, but I should use thee worse,
For thou I fear hast given me cause to curse.
If thou hast slain Lysander in his sleep,
Being o'er shoes in blood, plunge in the deep,
And kill me too.
The sun was not so true unto the day
As he to me. Would he have stolen away
From sleeping Hermia? I'll believe as soon
This whole earth may be bored, and that the moon
May through the centre creep, and so displease
Her brother's noontide with th'Antipodes.
It cannot be but thou hast murdered him.
So should a murderer look, so dead, so grim.

DEMETRIUS: So should the murdered look, and so should I,
Pierced through the heart with your stern cruelty.
Yet you the murderer look as bright, as clear
As yonder Venus in her glimmering sphere.

HERMIA: What's this to my Lysander, where is he?
　　Ah good Demetrius, wilt thou give him me?

DEMETRIUS: I had rather give his carcass to my hounds.

HERMIA: Out dog, out cur, thou driv'st me past the bounds
　　Of maiden's patience. Hast thou slain him then?
　　Henceforth be never numbered among men.
　　O once tell true; tell true, even for my sake.
　　Durst thou have looked upon him being awake,
　　And hast thou killed him sleeping? O brave touch!
　　Could not a worm, an adder do so much?
　　An adder did it, for with doubler tongue
　　Than thine, thou serpent, never adder stung.

DEMETRIUS: You spend your passion on a misprized mood.
　　I am not guilty of Lysander's blood,
　　Nor is he dead, for aught that I can tell.

HERMIA: I pray thee tell me then that he is well.

DEMETRIUS: And if I could, what should I get therefor?

HERMIA: A privilege never to see me more;
　　And from thy hated presence part I so.
　　See me no more, whether he be dead or no. (*Exit.*)

DEMETRIUS: There is no following her in this fierce vein.
　　Here therefore for a while I will remain.
　　So sorrow's heaviness doth heavier grow
　　For debt that bankrupt sleep doth sorrow owe,
　　Which now in some slight measure it will pay,
　　If for his tender here I make some stay. (*Lies down.*)

OBERON: What hast thou done? Thou hast mistaken quite,
　　And laid the love juice on some true love's sight.
　　Of thy misprision must perforce ensue
　　Some true love turned, and not a false turned true.

ROBIN: Then fate o'errules, that one man holding troth,
　　A million fail, confounding oath on oath.

OBERON: About the wood go swifter than the wind,
    And Helena of Athens look thou find.
    All fancy-sick she is, and pale of cheer,
    With sighs of love that costs the fresh blood dear.
    By some illusion see thou bring her here.
    I'll charm his eyes against she do appear.

ROBIN: I go, I go, look how I go,
    Swifter than arrow from the Tartar's bow. (*Exit.*)

OBERON: Flower of this purple dye,
    Hit with Cupid's archery,
    Sink in apple of his eye.
    When his love he doth espy,
    Let her shine as gloriously
    As the Venus of the sky.
    When thou wak'st, if she be by,
    Beg of her for remedy.

    Enter ROBIN.

ROBIN: Captain of our fairy band,
    Helena is here at hand,
    And the youth mistook by me,
    Pleading for a lover's fee.
    Shall we their fond pageant see?
    Lord, what fools these mortals be!

OBERON: Stand aside, the noise they make
    Will cause Demetrius to awake.

ROBIN: Then will two at once woo one.
    That must needs be sport alone;
    And those things do best please me
    That befall preposterously.

    Enter LYSANDER and HELENA.

LYSANDER:
    Why should you think that I should woo in scorn?
    Scorn and derision never come in tears.

Look when I vow I weep, and vows so born,
In their nativity all truth appears.
How can these things in me seem scorn to you,
Bearing the badge of faith to prove them true?

HELENA: You do advance your cunning more and more,
When truth kills truth, O devilish holy fray!
These vows are Hermia's, will you give her o'er?
Weigh oath with oath, and you will nothing weigh.
Your vows to her and me put in two scales
Will even weigh, and both as light as tales.

LYSANDER: I had no judgement when to her I swore.

HELENA: Nor none in my mind now you give her o'er.

LYSANDER: Demetrius loves her and he loves not you.

DEMETRIUS: (*Awakes.*)
O Helen, goddess, nymph, perfect, divine!
To what, my love, shall I compare thine eyne?
Crystal is muddy. O how ripe in show
Thy lips, those kissing cherries, tempting grow!
That pure congealèd white, high Taurus' snow,
Fanned with the eastern wind, turns to a crow
When thou hold'st up thy hand. O let me kiss
This princess of pure white, this seal of bliss!

HELENA: O spite! O hell! I see you all are bent
To set against me for your merriment.
If you were civil and knew courtesy,
You would not do me thus much injury.
Can you not hate me, as I know you do,
But you must join in souls to mock me too?
If you were men, as men you are in show,
You would not use a gentle lady so,
To vow and swear and superpraise my parts
When I am sure you hate me with your hearts.
You both are rivals and love Hermia,
And now both rivals to mock Helena.

A trim exploit, a manly enterprise,
To conjure tears up in a poor maid's eyes
With your derision. None of noble sort
Would so offend a virgin, and extort
A poor soul's patience, all to make you sport.

LYSANDER: You are unkind, Demetrius, be not so.
For you love Hermia, this you know I know.
And here with all good will, with all my heart,
In Hermia's love I yield you up my part;
And yours of Helena to me bequeath,
Whom I do love, and will do till my death.

HELENA: Never did mockers waste more idle breath.

DEMETRIUS: Lysander, keep thy Hermia, I will none.
If e'er I loved her, all that love is gone.
My heart to her but as guestwise sojourned
And now to Helen is it home returned,
There to remain.

LYSANDER: Helen, it is not so.

DEMETRIUS: Disparage not the faith thou dost not know,
Lest to thy peril thou aby it dear.
Look where thy love comes, yonder is thy dear.

Enter HERMIA.

HERMIA: Dark night, that from the eye his function takes,
The ear more quick of apprehension makes.
Wherein it doth impair the seeing sense,
It pays the hearing double recompense.
Thou art not by mine eye, Lysander, found;
Mine ear, I thank it, brought me to thy sound.
But why unkindly didst thou leave me so?

LYSANDER: Why should he stay whom love doth press to go?

HERMIA: What love could press Lysander from my side?

LYSANDER: Lysander's love, that would not let him bide:
    Fair Helena, who more engilds the night
    Than all yon fiery oes and eyes of light.
    Why seek'st thou me? Could not this make thee know
    The hate I bare thee made me leave thee so?

HERMIA: You speak not as you think, it cannot be.

HELENA: Lo, she is one of this confederacy.
    Now I perceive they have conjoined all three
    To fashion this false sport in spite of me.
    Injurious Hermia, most ungrateful maid,
    Have you conspired, have you with these contrived
    To bait me with this foul derision?
    Is all the counsel that we two have shared,
    The sisters' vows, the hours that we have spent
    When we have chid the hasty-footed time
    For parting us, O is all forgot?
    All schooldays' friendship, childhood innocence?
    We, Hermia, like two artificial gods
    Have with our needles created both one flower,
    Both on one sampler, sitting on one cushion,
    Both warbling of one song, both in one key,
    As if our hands, our sides, voices, and minds
    Had been incorporate. So we grew together,
    Like to a double cherry, seeming parted,
    But yet an union in partition,
    Two lovely berries moulded on one stem.
    So with two seeming bodies but one heart,
    Two of the first like coats in heraldry,
    Due but to one and crownèd with one crest.
    And will you rend our ancient love asunder,
    To join with men in scorning your poor friend?
    It is not friendly, 'tis not maidenly.
    Our sex as well as I may chide you for it,
    Though I alone do feel the injury.

HERMIA: I am amazèd at your passionate words.
    I scorn you not. It seems that you scorn me.

HELENA: Have you not set Lysander as in scorn
    To follow me and praise my eyes and face?
    And made your other love, Demetrius,
    Who even but now did spurn me with his foot,
    To call me goddess, nymph, divine, and rare,
    Precious, celestial? Wherefore speaks he this
    To her he hates? And wherefore doth Lysander
    Deny your love, so rich within his soul,
    And tender me, forsooth, affection,
    But by your setting on, by your consent?
    What though I be not so in grace as you,
    So hung upon with love, so fortunate,
    But miserable most, to love unloved?
    This you should pity rather than despise.

HERMIA: I understand not what you mean by this.

HELENA: Ay do persever, counterfeit sad looks,
    Make mouths upon me when I turn my back,
    Wink each at other, hold the sweet jest up.
    This sport well carried shall be chronicled.
    If you have any pity, grace or manners,
    You would not make me such an argument.
    But fare ye well, 'tis partly my own fault,
    Which death or absence soon shall remedy.

LYSANDER: Stay gentle Helena, hear my excuse,
    My love, my life, my soul, fair Helena.

HELENA: O excellent!

HERMIA: Sweet, do not scorn her so.

DEMETRIUS: If she cannot entreat I can compel.

LYSANDER: Thou canst compel no more than she entreat.
    Thy threats have no more strength than her weak prayers.

Helen I love thee, by my life I do.
I swear by that which I will lose for thee
To prove him false that says I love thee not.

DEMETRIUS: I say I love thee more than he can do.

LYSANDER: If thou say so, withdraw and prove it too.

DEMETRIUS: Quick, come.

HERMIA: Lysander, whereto tends all this?

LYSANDER: Away you Ethiope.

DEMETRIUS: No no sir,
Seem to break loose, take on as you would follow,
But yet come not, you are a tame man, go.

LYSANDER: Hang off, thou cat, thou burr, vile thing let loose,
Or I will shake thee from me like a serpent.

HERMIA: Why are you grown so rude? What change is this,
Sweet love?

LYSANDER: Thy love? Out tawny Tartar, out,
Out loathèd med'cine, O hated potion hence.

HERMIA: Do you not jest?

HELENA: Yes sooth, and so do you.

LYSANDER: Demetrius, I will keep my word with thee.

DEMETRIUS: I would I had your bond, for I perceive
A weak bond holds you. I'll not trust your word.

LYSANDER: What, should I hurt her, strike her, kill her dead?
Although I hate her, I'll not harm her so.

HERMIA: What, can you do me greater harm than hate?
Hate me, wherefore? O me, what news, my love?
Am not I Hermia? Are not you Lysander?
I am as fair now as I was erewhile.
Since night you loved me, yet since night you left me.

Why then you left me – O the gods forbid –
In earnest, shall I say?

LYSANDER: Ay, by my life,
And never did desire to see thee more.
Therefore be out of hope, of question, of doubt.
Be certain, nothing truer, 'tis no jest
That I do hate thee and love Helena.

HERMIA: O me, you juggler, you canker blossom,
You thief of love, what, have you come by night
And stolen my love's heart from him?

HELENA: Fine, i' faith.
Have you no modesty, no maiden shame,
No touch of bashfulness? What, will you tear
Impatient answers from my gentle tongue?
Fie fie, you counterfeit, you puppet, you!

HERMIA: Puppet? Why so, ay that way goes the game.
Now I perceive that she hath made compare
Between our statures, she hath urged her height,
And with her personage, her tall personage,
Her height, forsooth, she hath prevailed with him.
And are you grown so high in his esteem
Because I am so dwarfish and so low?
How low am I, thou painted maypole? Speak,
How low am I? I am not yet so low
But that my nails can reach unto thine eyes.

HELENA: I pray you, though you mock me, gentlemen,
Let her not hurt me. I was never curst,
I have no gift at all in shrewishness,
I am a right maid for my cowardice.
Let her not strike me. You perhaps may think
Because she is something lower than myself
That I can match her.

HERMIA: Lower? Hark again.

HELENA: Good Hermia, do not be so bitter with me.
　　I evermore did love you, Hermia,
　　Did ever keep your counsels, never wronged you,
　　Save that in love unto Demetrius
　　I told him of your stealth unto this wood.
　　He followed you, for love I followed him.
　　But he hath chid me hence, and threatened me
　　To strike me, spurn me, nay to kill me too.
　　And now, so you will let me quiet go,
　　To Athens will I bear my folly back,
　　And follow you no further. Let me go.
　　You see how simple and how fond I am.

HERMIA: Why get you gone, who is 't that hinders you?

HELENA: A foolish heart that I leave here behind.

HERMIA: What, with Lysander?

HELENA: 　　　　　　　　　　With Demetrius.

LYSANDER: Be not afraid, she shall not harm thee, Helena.

DEMETRIUS: No sir, she shall not, though you take her part.

HELENA: O when she is angry she is keen and shrewd,
　　She was a vixen when she went to school,
　　And though she be but little, she is fierce.

HERMIA: Little again, nothing but 'low' and 'little'?
　　Why will you suffer her to flout me thus?
　　Let me come to her.

LYSANDER: 　　　　　Get you gone, you dwarf,
　　You minimus of hindering knot-grass made,
　　You bead, you acorn.

DEMETRIUS: 　　　　　You are too officious
　　In her behalf that scorns your services.
　　Let her alone, speak not of Helena,
　　Take not her part, for if thou dost intend

Never so little show of love to her,
Thou shalt aby it.

LYSANDER: Now she holds me not.
Now follow, if thou dar'st, to try whose right,
Of thine or mine, is most in Helena.

DEMETRIUS: Follow? Nay, I'll go with thee, cheek by jowl.

Exeunt LYSANDER and DEMETRIUS.

HERMIA: You mistress, all this coil is long of you.
Nay go not back.

HELENA: I will not trust you, I,
Nor longer stay in your curst company.
Your hands than mine are quicker for a fray,
My legs are longer though, to run away. (*Exit.*)

HERMIA: I am amazed, and know not what to say. (*Exit.*)

OBERON: This is thy negligence, still thou mistak'st,
Or else committ'st thy knaveries wilfully.

ROBIN: Believe me, king of shadows, I mistook.
Did not you tell me I should know the man
By the Athenian garments he had on?
And so far blameless proves my enterprise
That I have 'nointed an Athenian's eyes;
And so far am I glad it so did sort
As this their jangling I esteem a sport.

OBERON: Thou seest these lovers seek a place to fight.
Hie therefore Robin, overcast the night;
The starry welkin cover thou anon
With drooping fog as black as Acheron,
And lead these testy rivals so astray
As one come not within another's way.
Like to Lysander sometime frame thy tongue,
Then stir Demetrius up with bitter wrong;
And sometime rail thou like Demetrius,

And from each other look thou lead them thus,
Till o'er their brows death-counterfeiting sleep
With leaden legs and batty wings doth creep.
Then crush this herb into Lysander's eye,
Whose liquor hath this virtuous property,
To take from thence all error with his might,
And make his eyeballs roll with wonted sight.
When they next wake, all this derision
Shall seem a dream and fruitless vision,
And back to Athens shall the lovers wend
With league whose date till death shall never end.
Whiles I in this affair do thee employ,
I'll to my queen and beg her Indian boy;
And then I will her charmèd eye release
From monster's view, and all things shall be peace.

ROBIN: My fairy lord, this must be done with haste,
For night's swift dragons cut the clouds full fast,
And yonder shines Aurora's harbinger,
At whose approach ghosts wandering here and there
Troop home to churchyards, damnèd spirits all
That in crossways and floods have burial,
Already to their wormy beds are gone,
For fear lest day should look their shames upon,
They wilfully themselves exile from light,
And must for aye consort with black-browed night.

OBERON: But we are spirits of another sort.
I with the morning's love have oft made sport,
And like a forester the groves may tread
Even till the eastern gate all fiery red,
Opening on Neptune with fair blessèd beams,
Turns into yellow gold his salt green streams.
But notwithstanding, haste, make no delay;
We may effect this business yet ere day. (*Exit.*)

ROBIN: Up and down, up and down,
I will lead them up and down.

I am feared in field and town.
Goblin, lead them up and down.
Here comes one.

Enter LYSANDER.

LYSANDER: Where art thou, proud Demetrius, speak thou
                                                                        now.

ROBIN: Here, villain, drawn and ready, where art thou?

LYSANDER: I will be with thee straight.

ROBIN: Follow me then
To plainer ground.

Exit LYSANDER.

Enter DEMETRIUS.

DEMETRIUS: Lysander, speak again.
Thou runaway, thou coward, art thou fled?
Speak, in some bush? Where dost thou hide thy head?

ROBIN: Thou coward, art thou bragging to the stars,
Telling the bushes that thou look'st for wars,
And wilt not come? Come recreant, come thou child,
I'll whip thee with a rod, he is defiled
That draws a sword on thee.

DEMETRIUS: Yea, art thou there?

ROBIN: Follow my voice, we'll try no manhood here.

Exeunt ROBIN and DEMETRIUS.

Enter LYSANDER.

LYSANDER: He goes before me and still dares me on;
When I come where he calls, then he is gone.
The villain is much lighter heeled than I;
I followed fast, but faster he did fly,
That fallen am I in dark uneven way,

And here will rest me. (*Lies down.*) Come thou gentle day,
For if but once thou show me thy grey light,
I'll find Demetrius, and revenge this spite.

Enter ROBIN and DEMETRIUS.

ROBIN: Ho ho ho coward, why com'st thou not?

DEMETRIUS: Abide me if thou dar'st, for well I wot
Thou runn'st before me, shifting every place,
And dar'st not stand nor look me in the face.
Where art thou now?

ROBIN: Come hither, I am here.

DEMETRIUS:
Nay then thou mock'st me. Thou shalt buy this dear
If ever I thy face by daylight see.
Now go thy way, faintness constraineth me
To measure out my length on this cold bed.
By day's approach look to be visited. (*Lies down.*)

Enter HELENA.

HELENA: O weary night, O long and tedious night,
Abate thy hours, shine comforts from the east,
That I may back to Athens by daylight
From these that my poor company detest.
And sleep, that sometimes shuts up sorrow's eye,
Steal me a while from mine own company. (*Sleeps.*)

ROBIN: Yet but three? Come one more,
Two of both kinds makes up four.
Here she comes, curst and sad.
Cupid is a knavish lad
Thus to make poor females mad.

Enter HERMIA.

HERMIA: Never so weary, never so in woe,
Bedabbled with the dew, and torn with briars,

I can no further crawl, no further go.
My legs can keep no pace with my desires.
Here will I rest me till the break of day.
Heavens shield Lysander, if they mean a fray. (*Sleeps.*)

ROBIN: On the ground sleep sound.
I'll apply to your eye,
Gentle lover, remedy.
When thou wak'st thou tak'st
True delight in the sight
Of thy former lady's eye,
And the country proverb known,
That every man should take his own,
In your waking shall be shown.
Jack shall have Jill,
Naught shall go ill,
The man shall have his mare again, and all shall be well.
(*Exit.*)

Scene Seven

Enter TITANIA, BOTTOM, and FAIRIES, and OBERON behind them.

TITANIA: Come sit thee down upon this flowery bed,
While I thy amiable cheeks do coy,
And stick musk-roses in thy sleek smooth head,
And kiss thy fair large ears, my gentle joy.

BOTTOM: Where's Peaseblossom?

PEASEBLOSSOM: Ready.

BOTTOM: Scratch my head, Peaseblossom. Where's mounsieur Cobweb?

COBWEB: Ready.

BOTTOM: Mounsieur Cobweb, good mounsieur, get you your weapons in your hand and kill me a red-hipped

humble-bee on the top of a thistle, and good mounsieur, bring me the honeybag. Do not fret yourself too much in the action, mounsieur; and good mounsieur, have a care the honeybag break not. I would be loath to have you overflown with a honeybag, signor. Where's mounsieur Mustardseed?

MUSTARDSEED: Ready.

BOTTOM: Give me your neaf, mounsieur Mustardseed. Pray you leave your courtesy, good mounsieur.

MUSTARDSEED: What's your will?

BOTTOM: Nothing, good mounsieur, but to help Cavaliery Cobweb to scratch. I must to the barber's, mounsieur, for methinks I am marvellous hairy about the face, and I am such a tender ass, if my hair do but tickle me I must scratch.

TITANIA: What, wilt thou hear some music, my sweet love?

BOTTOM: I have a reasonable good ear in music. Let's have the tongs and the bones.

TITANIA: Or say, sweet love, what thou desir'st to eat.

BOTTOM: Truly, a peck of provender. I could munch your good dry oats. Methinks I have a great desire to a bottle of hay. Good hay, sweet hay, hath no fellow.

TITANIA: I have a venturous fairy that shall seek The squirrel's hoard, and fetch thee new nuts.

BOTTOM: I had rather have a handful or two of dried peas. But I pray you, let none of your people stir me, I have an exposition of sleep come upon me.

TITANIA: Sleep thou, and I will wind thee in my arms. Fairies be gone, and be all ways away.

Exeunt FAIRIES.

So doth the woodbine the sweet honeysuckle
Gently entwist; the female ivy so
Enrings the barky fingers of the elm.
O how I love thee, how I dote on thee!

Enter ROBIN GOODFELLOW.

OBERON: Welcome good Robin, seest thou this sweet sight?
Her dotage now I do begin to pity,
For meeting her of late behind the wood,
Seeking sweet favours for this hateful fool,
I did upbraid her and fall out with her,
For she his hairy temples then had rounded
With coronet of fresh and fragrant flowers,
And that same dew which sometime on the buds
Was wont to swell like round and orient pearls
Stood now within the pretty flowerets' eyes,
Like tears that did their own disgrace bewail.
When I had at my pleasure taunted her,
And she in mild terms begged my patience,
I then did ask of her her changeling child,
Which straight she gave me, and her fairy sent
To bear him to my bower in fairyland.
And now I have the boy, I will undo
This hateful imperfection of her eyes.
And gentle puck, take this transformèd scalp
From off the head of this Athenian swain,
That he awaking when the other do,
May all to Athens back again repair,
And think no more of this night's accidents
But as the fierce vexation of a dream.
But first I will release the fairy queen.
Be as thou wast wont to be,
See as thou wast wont to see.
Dian's bud o'er Cupid's flower
Hath such force and blessèd power.
Now my Titania, wake you, my sweet queen.

TITANIA: My Oberon, what visions have I seen!
   Methought I was enamoured of an ass.

OBERON: There lies your love.

TITANIA: How came these things to
                                                           pass?

   O how mine eyes do loathe his visage now!

OBERON: Silence a while. Robin, take off this head.
   Titania, music call, and strike more dead
   Than common sleep of all these five the sense.

TITANIA: Music ho, music such as charmeth sleep.

ROBIN: Now when thou wak'st, with thine own fool's eyes
                                                           peep.

OBERON: Sound music.

   Still music.

   Come my queen, take hands with me,
   And rock the ground whereon these sleepers be.
   Now thou and I are new in amity,
   And will tomorrow midnight solemnly
   Dance in Duke Theseus' house triumphantly,
   And bless it to all fair prosperity.
   There shall the pairs of faithful lovers be
   Wedded with Theseus, all in jollity.

ROBIN: Fairy king, attend and mark.
   I do hear the morning lark.

OBERON: Then my queen, in silence sad
   Trip we after the night's shade.
   We the globe can compass soon,
   Swifter than the wandering moon.

TITANIA: Come my lord, and in our flight
   Tell me how it came this night

That I sleeping here was found
With these mortals on the ground.

Exeunt FAIRIES.

*Wind horns within. Enter THESEUS with HIPPOLYTA,
EGEUS, and all his train.*

THESEUS: Go one of you, find out the forester,
For now our observation is performed,
And since we have the vaward of the day,
My love shall hear the music of my hounds.
Uncouple in the western valley, let them go.
Dispatch I say, and find the forester.
We will, fair queen, up to the mountain's top,
And mark the musical confusion
Of hounds and echo in conjunction.

HIPPOLYTA: I was with Hercules and Cadmus once
When in a wood of Crete they bayed the bear
With hounds of Sparta. Never did I hear
Such gallant chiding, for besides the groves,
The skies, the fountains, every region near
Seemed all one mutual cry. I never heard
So musical a discord, such sweet thunder.

THESEUS: My hounds are bred out of the Spartan kind,
So flewed, so sanded, and their heads are hung
With ears that sweep away the morning dew,
Crook-kneed, and dewlapped like Thessalian bulls;
Slow in pursuit, but matched in mouth like bells,
Each under each. A cry more tuneable
Was never hollered to nor cheered with horn
In Crete, in Sparta, nor in Thessaly.
Judge when you hear. But soft, what nymphs are these?

EGEUS: My lord, this is my daughter here asleep,
And this Lysander, this Demetrius is,
This Helena, old Nedar's Helena.
I wonder of their being here together.

THESEUS: No doubt they rose up early to observe
    The rite of May; and hearing our intent,
    Came here in grace of our solemnity.
    But speak Egeus, is not this the day
    That Hermia should give answer of her choice?

EGEUS: It is, my lord.

THESEUS: Go bid the huntsmen wake them with their horns.

Shout within. Wind horns. The lovers all start up.

    Good morrow friends, Saint Valentine is past.
    Begin these woodbirds but to couple now?

LYSANDER: Pardon, my lord.

THESEUS: I pray you all stand up.
    I know you two are rival enemies.
    How comes this gentle concord in the world,
    That hatred is so far from jealousy
    To sleep by hate, and fear no enmity?

LYSANDER: My lord, I shall reply amazedly,
    Half sleep, half waking, but as yet I swear
    I cannot truly say how I came here,
    But as I think, for truly would I speak,
    And now I do bethink me so it is,
    I came with Hermia hither. Our intent
    Was to be gone from Athens, where we might,
    Without the peril of the Athenian law –

EGEUS: Enough enough, my lord, you have enough.
    I beg the law, the law upon his head.
    They would have stolen away, they would, Demetrius,
    Thereby to have defeated you and me,
    You of your wife, and me of my consent,
    Of my consent that she should be your wife.

DEMETRIUS: My lord, fair Helen told me of their stealth,
    Of this their purpose hither to this wood,

And I in fury hither followed them,
Fair Helena in fancy following me.
But my good lord, I wot not by what power,
But by some power it is, my love to Hermia,
Melted as the snow, seems to me now
As the remembrance of an idle gaud
Which in my childhood I did dote upon,
And all the faith, the virtue of my heart,
The object and the pleasure of mine eye
Is only Helena. To her, my lord,
Was I betrothed ere I saw Hermia.
But like in sickness did I loathe this food,
But as in health, come to my natural taste,
Now I do wish it, love it, long for it,
And will for evermore be true to it.

THESEUS: Fair lovers, you are fortunately met.
Of this discourse we more will hear anon.
Egeus, I will overbear your will,
For in the temple by and by with us
These couples shall eternally be knit.
And for the morning now is something worn,
Our purposed hunting shall be set aside.
Away with us to Athens. Three and three
We'll hold a feast in great solemnity.
Come, Hippolyta.

Exit THESEUS with HIPPOLYTA, EGEUS, and train.

DEMETRIUS: These things seem small and undistinguishable,
Like far-off mountains turnèd into clouds.

HERMIA: Methinks I see these things with parted eye,
When everything seems double.

HELENA: So methinks,
And I have found Demetrius like a jewel,
Mine own and not mine own.

DEMETRIUS: Are you sure
  That we are awake? It seems to me
  That yet we sleep, we dream. Do not you think
  The Duke was here and bid us follow him?

HERMIA: Yea, and my father.

HELENA: And Hippolyta.

LYSANDER: And he did bid us follow to the temple.

DEMETRIUS: Why then, we are awake. Let's follow him,
  And by the way let us recount our dreams.

Exeunt lovers. BOTTOM wakes.

BOTTOM: When my cue comes, call me, and I will answer.
  My next is 'most fair Pyramus'. Hey-ho. Peter Quince?
  Flute the bellows-mender? Snout the tinker? Starveling?
  God's my life, stolen hence, and left me asleep? I have
  had a most rare vision. I have had a dream past the wit
  of man to say what dream it was. Man is but an ass if he
  go about to expound this dream. Methought I was –
  there is no man can tell what. Methought I was, and
  methought I had – but man is but a patched fool if he
  will offer to say what methought I had. The eye of man
  hath not heard, the ear of man hath not seen, man's hand
  is not able to taste, his tongue to conceive, nor his heart
  to report what my dream was. I will get Peter Quince to
  write a ballad of this dream. It shall be called 'Bottom's
  Dream', because it hath no bottom; and I will sing it in
  the latter end of a play before the Duke. Peradventure, to
  make it the more gracious, I shall sing it at her death.
  (*Exit.*)

Scene Eight

Enter QUINCE, FLUTE, SNOUT, and STARVELING.

QUINCE: Have you sent to Bottom's house? Is he come home yet?

STARVELING: He cannot be heard of. Out of doubt he is transported.

FLUTE: If he come not, then the play is marred. It goes not forward. Doth it?

QUINCE: It is not possible. You have not a man in all Athens able to discharge Pyramus but he.

FLUTE: No, he hath simply the best wit of any handicraft-man in Athens.

QUINCE: Yea, and the best person, too; and he is a very paramour for a sweet voice.

FLUTE: You must say 'paragon'. A paramour is, God bless us, a thing of naught.

Enter SNUG the joiner.

SNUG: Masters, the Duke is coming from the temple, and there is two or three lords and ladies more married. If our sport had gone forward we had all been made men.

FLUTE: O sweet bully Bottom, thus hath he lost sixpence a day during his life. He could not have scaped sixpence a day. An the Duke had not given him sixpence a day for playing Pyramus, I'll be hanged. He would have deserved it. Sixpence a day in Pyramus, or nothing.

Enter BOTTOM.

BOTTOM: Where are these lads? Where are these hearts?

QUINCE: Bottom! O most courageous day! O most happy hour!

BOTTOM: Masters, I am to discourse wonders; but ask me not what, for if I tell you, I am no true Athenian. I will tell you everything right as it fell out.

QUINCE: Let us hear, sweet Bottom.

BOTTOM: Not a word of me. All that I will tell you is that the Duke hath dined. Get your apparel together, good strings to your beards, new ribbons to your pumps, meet presently at the palace, every man look o'er his part. For the short and the long is, our play is preferred. In any case let Thisbe have clean linen, and let not him that plays the lion pare his nails, for they shall hang out for the lion's claws. And most dear actors, eat no onions nor garlic, for we are to utter sweet breath, and I do not doubt but to hear them say it is a sweet comedy. No more words. Away, go away!

Exeunt.

Scene Nine

Enter THESEUS and HIPPOLYTA.

HIPPOLYTA: 'Tis strange, my Theseus, that these lovers
speak of.

THESEUS: More strange than true. I never may believe
These antique fables nor these fairy toys.
Lovers and madmen have such seething brains,
Such shaping fantasies, that apprehend
More than cool reason ever comprehends.
The lunatic, the lover, and the poet
Are of imagination all compact.
One sees more devils than vast hell can hold:
That is the madman. The lover, all as frantic,
Sees Helen's beauty in a brow of Egypt.
The poet's eye, in a fine frenzy rolling,
Doth glance from heaven to earth, from earth to heaven,

And as imagination bodies forth
The forms of things unknown, the poet's pen
Turns them to shapes, and gives to airy nothing
A local habitation and a name.
Such tricks hath strong imagination
That if it would but apprehend some joy
It comprehends some bringer of that joy;
Or in the night, imagining some fear,
How easy is a bush supposed a bear!

HIPPOLYTA: But all the story of the night told over,
And all their minds transfigured so together,
More witnesseth than fancy's images,
And grows to something of great constancy;
But howsoever, strange and admirable.

Enter the lovers: LYSANDER, DEMETRIUS, HERMIA, and HELENA.

THESEUS: Here come the lovers, full of joy and mirth.
Joy, gentle friends, joy and fresh days of love
Accompany your hearts.

LYSANDER: More than to us
Wait in your royal walks, your board, your bed.

THESEUS: Come now, what masques, what dances shall
                                        we have
To wear away this long age of three hours
Between our after-supper and bed-time?
Where is our usual manager of mirth?
What revels are in hand, is there no play
To ease the anguish of a torturing hour?
Say what abridgement have you for this evening,
What masque, what music? How shall we beguile
The lazy time if not with some delight?

HIPPOLYTA: There is a brief how many sports are ripe.
Make choice of which your highness will see first.

THESEUS: (*Reads.*) 'The battle with the centaurs, to be sung
By an Athenian eunuch to the harp.'
We'll none of that. That have I told my love
In glory of my kinsman Hercules.

HIPPOLYTA: (*Reads.*) 'The riot of the tipsy bacchanals
Tearing the Thracian singer in their rage.'

THESEUS: That is an old device, and it was played
When I from Thebes came last a conqueror.

HERMIA: (*Reads.*)
'The thrice-three muses mourning for the death
Of learning, late deceased in beggary.'

THESEUS: That is some satire, keen and critical,
Not sorting with a nuptial ceremony.

HELENA: (*Reads.*) 'A tedious brief scene of young Pyramus
And his love Thisbe: very tragical mirth.'

THESEUS: Merry and tragical? Tedious and brief?
That is hot ice and wondrous strange snow.
How shall we find the concord of this discord?

HIPPOLYTA: A play there is, my lord, some ten words long,
Which is as brief as I have known a play;
But by ten words, my lord, it is too long,
Which makes it tedious; for in all the play
There is not one word apt, one player fitted.
And tragical, my noble lord, it is,
For Pyramus therein doth kill himself.
Which when I saw rehearsed I must confess,
Made mine eyes water, but more merry tears
The passion of loud laughter never shed.

THESEUS: What are they that do play it?

HIPPOLYTA: Hard-handed men that work in Athens here,
Which never laboured in their minds till now,
And now have toiled their unbreathed memories
With this same play against your nuptial.

THESEUS: And we will hear it.

HIPPOLYTA: No my noble lord,
   It is not for you. I have heard it over,
   And it is nothing, nothing in the world,
   Unless you can find sport in their intents
   Extremely stretched and conned with cruel pain
   To do you service.

THESEUS: I will hear that play;
   For never anything can be amiss
   When simpleness and duty tender it.
   Go bring them in; and take your places, ladies.

HIPPOLYTA: I love not to see wretchedness o'ercharged,
   And duty in his service perishing.

THESEUS: Why gentle sweet, you shall see no such thing.

HIPPOLYTA: I know they can do nothing in this kind.

THESEUS: The kinder we, to give them thanks for nothing.
   Our sport shall be to take what they mistake,
   And what poor duty cannot do,
   Noble respect takes it in might, not merit.
   Where I have come, great clerks have purposèd
   To greet me with premeditated welcomes,
   Where I have seen them shiver and look pale,
   Make periods in the midst of sentences,
   Throttle their practised accent in their fears,
   And in conclusion dumbly have broke off,
   Not paying me a welcome. Trust me, sweet,
   Out of this silence yet I picked a welcome,
   And in the modesty of fearful duty
   I read as much as from the rattling tongue
   Of saucy and audacious eloquence.
   Love, therefore, and tongue-tied simplicity
   In least speak most, to my capacity.

LYSANDER: So please your grace, the Prologue is addressed.

THESEUS: Let him approach.

Enter QUINCE as Prologue.

QUINCE: If we offend it is with our good will.
    That you should think we come not to offend
    But with good will. To show our simple skill,
    That is the true beginning of our end.
    Consider then we come but in despite.
    We do not come as minding to content you,
    Our true intent is. All for your delight
    We are not here. That you should here repent you
    The actors are at hand, and by their show
    You shall know all that you are like to know.

THESEUS: This fellow doth not stand upon points.

LYSANDER: He hath rid his prologue like a rough colt: he
    knows not the stop. A good moral, my lord: it is not
    enough to speak, but to speak true.

HIPPOLYTA: Indeed, he hath played on his prologue like
    a child on a recorder: a sound, but not in government.

THESEUS: His speech was like a tangled chain, nothing
    impaired but all disordered. Who is next?

*Enter BOTTOM as Pyramus, FLUTE as Thisbe, SNOUT as
Wall, STARVELING as Moonshine, and SNUG as Lion.*

QUINCE: Gentles, perchance you wonder at this show,
    But wonder on, till truth make all things plain.
    This man is Pyramus, if you would know;
    This beauteous lady Thisbe is certain.
    This man with lime and roughcast doth present
    Wall, that vile wall which did these lovers sunder;
    And through Wall's chink, poor souls, they are content
    To whisper, at the which let no man wonder.
    This man with lantern, dog, and bush of thorn,
    Presenteth Moonshine, for if you will know,

By moonshine did these lovers think no scorn
To meet at Ninus' tomb, there, there to woo.
This grizzly beast, which Lion hight by name,
The trusty Thisbe coming first by night
Did scare away, or rather did affright,
And as she fled, her mantle she did fall,
Which Lion vile with bloody mouth did stain.
Anon comes Pyramus, sweet youth and tall,
And finds his trusty Thisbe's mantle slain;
Whereat with blade, with bloody blameful blade,
He bravely broached his boiling bloody breast;
And Thisbe, tarrying in mulberry shade,
His dagger drew and died. For all the rest,
Let Lion, Moonshine, Wall, and lovers twain
At large discourse while here they do remain.

Exeunt all but SNOUT as Wall.

THESEUS: I wonder if the lion be to speak.

HELENA: No wonder my lord, one lion may when many
    asses do.

SNOUT: In this same interlude it doth befall
    That I, one Snout by name, present a wall,
    And such a wall as I would have you think
    That had in it a crannied hole or chink,
    Through which the lovers Pyramus and Thisbe
    Did whisper often very secretly.
    This loam, this roughcast, and this stone doth show
    That I am that same wall, the truth is so.
    And this the cranny is, right and sinister,
    Through which the fearful lovers are to whisper.

THESEUS: Would you desire lime and hair to speak better?

HELENA: It is the wittiest partition that ever I heard
    discourse, my lord.

Enter BOTTOM as Pyramus.

THESEUS: Pyramus draws near the wall. Silence.

BOTTOM: O grim-looked night, O night with hue so black,
    O night which ever art when day is not;
    O night O night, alack alack alack,
    I fear my Thisbe's promise is forgot.
    And thou O wall, O sweet O lovely wall,
    That stand'st between her father's ground and mine,
    Thou wall, O wall, O sweet and lovely wall,
    Show me thy chink, to blink through with mine eyne.
    Thanks courteous wall, Jove shield thee well for this.
    But what see I? No Thisbe do I see.
    O wicked wall, through whom I see no bliss,
    Cursed be thy stones for thus deceiving me.

THESEUS: The wall methinks being sensible should curse
    again.

BOTTOM: No in truth sir, he should not. 'Deceiving me' is
    Thisbe's cue: she is to enter now, and I am to spy her
    through the wall. You shall see it will fall pat as I told
    you: yonder she comes.

Enter FLUTE as Thisbe.

FLUTE: O wall, full often hast thou heard my moans
    For parting my fair Pyramus and me.
    My cherry lips have often kissed thy stones,
    Thy stones with lime and hair knit up in thee.

BOTTOM: I see a voice. Now will I to the chink
    To spy an I can hear my Thisbe's face.
    Thisbe?

FLUTE: My love – thou art my love, I think.

BOTTOM: Think what thou wilt, I am thy lover's grace,
    And like Limander am I trusty still.

FLUTE: And I like Helen, till the fates me kill.

BOTTOM: Not Shafalus to Procrus was so true.

FLUTE: As Shafalus to Procrus, I to you.

BOTTOM: O kiss me through the hole of this vile wall.

FLUTE: I kiss the wall's hole, not your lips at all.

BOTTOM: Wilt thou at Ninny's tomb meet me straightway?

FLUTE: Tide life, tide death, I come without delay.

Exeunt BOTTOM and FLUTE.

SNOUT: Thus have I, Wall, my part dischargèd so;
And being done, thus Wall away doth go. (*Exit.*)

THESEUS: Now is the mural down between the two
neighbours.

HELENA: No remedy, my lord, when walls are so wilful to
hear without warning.

HIPPOLYTA: This is the silliest stuff that ever I heard.

THESEUS: The best in this kind are but shadows, and the
worst are no worse if imagination amend them.

HIPPOLYTA: It must be your imagination then, and not
theirs.

THESEUS: If we imagine no worse of them than they of
themselves, they may pass for excellent men. Here come
two noble beasts in, a moon and a lion.

Enter SNUG as Lion and STARVELING as Moonshine.

SNUG: You ladies you whose gentle hearts do fear
The smallest monstrous mouse that creeps on floor,
May now perchance both quake and tremble here
When lion rough in wildest rage doth roar.
Then know that I one Snug the joiner am
A lion fell, nor else no lion's dam.
For if I should as Lion come in strife
Into this place, 'twere pity on my life.

THESEUS: A very gentle beast, and of a good conscience.

HIPPOLYTA: The very best at a beast, my lord, that e'er I saw.

LYSANDER: This lion is a very fox for his valour.

THESEUS: True, and a goose for his discretion.

HELENA: Not so, my lord, for his valour cannot carry his discretion, and the fox carries the goose.

THESEUS: His discretion, I am sure, cannot carry his valour, for the goose carries not the fox. It is well. Leave it to his discretion, and let us listen to the moon.

STARVELING: This lanthorn doth the hornèd moon present.

LYSANDER: He should have worn the horns on his head.

THESEUS: He is no crescent, and his horns are invisible within the circumference.

STARVELING: This lanthorn doth the hornèd moon present. Myself the man i' th' moon do seem to be.

THESEUS: This is the greatest error of all the rest: the man should be put into the lantern. How is it else the man i' th' moon?

LYSANDER: He dares not come there for the candle; for you see it is already in snuff.

HIPPOLYTA: I am aweary of this moon, would he would change.

THESEUS: It appears by his small light of discretion that he is in the wane; but yet in courtesy, in all reason, we must stay the time.

LYSANDER: Proceed, Moon.

STARVELING: All that I have to say is to tell you that the lantern is the moon, I the man i' th' moon, this thorn bush my thorn bush, and this dog my dog.

HELENA: Why, all these should be in the lantern, for all these are in the moon.

HIPPOLYTA: But silence; here comes Thisbe.

Enter FLUTE as Thisbe.

FLUTE: This is old Ninny's tomb. Where is my love?

SNUG: (*Roars.*) Oh!

Thisbe runs off.

LYSANDER: Well roared, Lion.

THESEUS: Well run, Thisbe.

HIPPOLYTA: Well shone, Moon. Truly, the moon shines with a good grace.

THESEUS: Well moused, Lion.

HELENA: And then came Pyramus.

LYSANDER: And so the lion vanished.

Enter BOTTOM as Pyramus. Exit SNUG as Lion.

BOTTOM: Sweet moon, I thank thee for thy sunny beams.
I thank thee, moon, for shining now so bright;
For by thy gracious, golden, glittering gleams
I trust to take of truest Thisbe sight.
But stay, O spite!
But mark, poor knight,
What dreadful dole is here?
Eyes, do you see?
How can it be?
O dainty duck, O dear!
Thy mantle good,

What, stained with blood?
Approach, ye furies fell.
O fates, come come,
Cut thread and thrum,
Quail, crush, conclude, and quell.

THESEUS: This passion and the death of a dear friend
would go near to make a man look sad.

HIPPOLYTA: Beshrew my heart, but I pity the man.

BOTTOM: O wherefore, nature, didst thou lions frame,
Since lion vile hath here deflowered my dear?
Which is, no no which was, the fairest dame
That lived, that loved, that liked, that looked, with cheer.
Come tears, confound;
Out sword, and wound
The pap of Pyramus,
Ay, that left pap,
Where heart doth hop.
Thus die I: thus, thus, thus.
Now am I dead,
Now am I fled,
My soul is in the sky.
Tongue, lose thy light;
Moon, take thy flight.

Exit STARVELING as Moonshine.

Now die, die, die, die, die.

DEMETRIUS: No die but an ace for him; for he is but one.

LYSANDER: Less than an ace, man; for he is dead; he is
nothing.

THESEUS: With the help of a surgeon he might yet
recover and prove an ass.

HIPPOLYTA: How chance Moonshine is gone before
Thisbe comes back and finds her lover?

Enter FLUTE as Thisbe.

THESEUS: She will find him by starlight.
Here she comes, and her passion ends the play.

HIPPOLYTA: Methinks she should not use a long one for such a Pyramus. I hope she will be brief.

DEMETRIUS: A mote will turn the balance which Pyramus, which Thisbe, is the better: he for a man, God warrant us, she for a woman, God bless us.

LYSANDER: She hath spied him already with those sweet eyes.

DEMETRIUS: And thus she means, videlicet.

FLUTE: Asleep, my love?
What, dead, my dove?
O Pyramus, arise.
Speak, speak. Quite dumb?
Dead, dead? A tomb
Must cover thy sweet eyes.
These lily lips,
This cherry nose,
These yellow cowslip cheeks
Are gone, are gone.
Lovers, make moan.
His eyes were green as leeks.
O sisters three,
Come come to me
With hands as pale as milk.
Lay them in gore,
Since you have shore
With shears his thread of silk.
Tongue, not a word.
Come trusty sword,
Come blade, my breast imbrue.
And farewell friends,

Thus Thisbe ends.
Adieu, adieu, adieu.

THESEUS: Moonshine and Lion are left to bury the dead.

DEMETRIUS: Ay, and Wall too.

BOTTOM: No I assure you, the wall is down that parted
their fathers. Will it please you to see the epilogue or to
hear a bergamask dance between two of our company?

THESEUS: No epilogue, I pray you, for your play needs
no excuse. Never excuse, for when the players are all
dead there need none to be blamed. Marry, if he that writ
it had played Pyramus and hanged himself in Thisbe's
garter it would have been a fine tragedy; and so it is
truly, and very notably discharged. But come, your
bergamask. Let your epilogue alone.

Dance. Exeunt Mechanicals.

The iron tongue of midnight hath told twelve.
Lovers to bed, 'tis almost fairy time.
I fear we shall outsleep the coming morn
As much as we this night have overwatched.
This palpable-gross play hath well beguiled
The heavy gait of night. Sweet friends, to bed.
A fortnight hold we this solemnity
In nightly revels and new jollity.

Exeunt.

Enter ROBIN GOODFELLOW.

ROBIN: Now the hungry lion roars,
    And the wolf behowls the moon,
    Whilst the heavy ploughman snores,
    All with weary task fordone.
    Now the wasted brands do glow
    Whilst the screech-owl screeching loud
    Puts the wretch that lies in woe

In remembrance of a shroud.
Now it is the time of night
That the graves all gaping wide,
Every one lets forth his sprite
In the churchway paths to glide;
And we fairies that do run
By the triple Hecate's team
From the presence of the sun,
Following darkness like a dream,
Now are frolic. Not a mouse
Shall disturb this hallowed house.
I am sent with broom before
To sweep the dust behind the door.

Enter OBERON and TITANIA, with all their train.

OBERON: Through the house give glimmering light.
By the dead and drowsy fire
Every elf and fairy sprite
Hop as light as bird from briar,
And this ditty after me
Sing and dance it trippingly.

TITANIA: First rehearse your song by rote,
To each word a warbling note.
Hand in hand with fairy grace
Will we sing and bless this place.

OBERON: Now until the break of day
Through this house each fairy stray.
To the best bride bed will we,
Which by us shall blessèd be,
And the issue there create
Ever shall be fortunate.
So shall all the couples three
Ever true in loving be,
And the blots of nature's hand
Shall not in their issue stand.

Never mole, harelip, nor scar,
Nor mark prodigious such as are
Despisèd in nativity
Shall upon their children be.
With this field-dew consecrate
Every fairy take his gait
And each several chamber bless
Through this palace with sweet peace;
And the owner of it blest
Ever shall in safety rest.
Trip away, make no stay,
Meet me all by break of day.

Exeunt all but ROBIN.

ROBIN: If we shadows have offended,
Think but this and all is mended,
That you have but slumbered here,
While these visions did appear;
And this weak and idle theme,
No more yielding but a dream,
Gentles, do not reprehend.
If you pardon, we will mend.
And as I am an honest puck,
If we have unearnèd luck
Now to scape the serpent's tongue,
We will make amends ere long,
Else the puck a liar call.
So good night unto you all.
Give me your hands if we be friends,
And Robin shall restore amends. (*Exit.*)